Grace

The Reality of Redemption

Grace

The Reality of Redemption

Jannah A. Mitchell

ARPress LLC
45 Dan Road Suite 5
Canton MA 02021
Hotline: 1(888) 821-0229
Fax: 1(508) 545-7580

Ordering Information:
Quantity sales. Special discounts are available on quantity purchases by corporations, associations, and others. For details, contact the publisher at the address above.

Printed in the United States of America.

ISBN-13:   Softcover   979-8-89330-723-8
                    eBook   979-8-89330-724-5

Library of Congress Control Number: 2024902477

DEDICATION

I would like to dedicate this book to Cynthia Morrow and the members of the Priscilla House of Faith Prayer Group. They prayed me through the writing of this book. I gratefully acknowledge my son and daughter, Hajji and Angel, -- who have cared for me so kindly and selflessly during this period of health challenges. All praise is due to Almighty God for His love, mercy, grace and faithfulness throughout my lifetime. I worship and adore my heavenly Father. I look forward to fellowship with all of you here on earth and in heaven.

Contents

PREFACE

Man was created to live in God's presence. Outside of God's presence man is incomplete and lost and miserable. Adam and Eve were placed in a garden on the east side of Eden (Genesis 2:8). God visited Adam and Eve in the cool of the day (Genesis 3:8).

The Tree of Life and the Tree of the Knowledge of Good and Evil were also planted in Adam's garden. God commanded Adam not to eat of the Tree of the Knowledge of Good and Evil. If Adam did so, he would surely die (Genesis 2:16- 17).

To live in God's presence is life. To live outside of God's presence is misery and death. When Adam and Eve disobeyed God, by eating of the Tree of the Knowledge of Good and Evil, they were punished with separation from God. They were banned from the heavenly Garden of Eden and assigned to making a living and bearing children on their own. The greatest punishment was their separation from God – a curse passed down to mankind throughout the ages. (Genesis 3:16- 19)

"For as by one man's disobedience many were made sinncrs, so by the obedience of one shall many be made righteous." (Romans 5:19)

Through the disobedience of Adam (one man), we were all made sinners. But through the blood sacrifice and obedience of Jesus Christ, we received the gift of grace and salvation from sin. We only need to accept the gift.

"But not as the offence, so also is the free gift. For if through the offence of one many be dead, much more the grace of God, and the gift by grace, which is by one man, Jesus Christ, hath abounded unto many." (Romans 5:15)

The entirety of the scriptures, following the fall of mankind, addresses the long trek back to the presence of God. The universe held legal requirements for the redemption of man to his original state of innocence and sinlessness. In order to gain that ethereal reward, blood had to be shed.

The act of one man introduced the curse. The act of another man paid the price to redeem mankind from that curse.

Hebrews 9:22 states clearly: **"And almost all things are by the law purged with blood; and without shedding of blood is no remission."** Throughout the Old Testament (the Old Covenant) the high priests of the Levites were assigned the task of offering blood sacrifices, for the errors of themselves and the errors of the people. (Hebrews 9:7) Hebrews 9:9 states that these sacrifices and gifts did not make the high priest perfect "as pertaining to the conscience". The conscience still retained the imprint of sin and the regret/remorse associated with it. Under the old covenant, man could never stand in the Father's presence without a sense of guilt or inferiority. Man could never obey each and every law and rule set before him in those times, and not even the sacrifices could clean his conscience completely.

Jesus' death and resurrection created a New Testament (New Covenant). Hebrews 9:13-17 reads: **"For if the blood of bulls and of goats, and the ashes of an heifer sprinkling the unclean, sanctifieth to the purifying of the flesh;**

How much more shall the blood of Christ, who through the eternal Spirit offered himself without spot to God, purge your conscience from dead works to serve the living God.

And for this cause he is the mediator of the new testament, that by means of death, for the redemption of the transgressions that were under the first testament, they which are called might receive the promise of eternal inheritance.

For where a testament is, there must also of necessity be the death of the testator.

For a testament is of force after men are dead: otherwise it is of no strength at all while the testator liveth."

Under the Old Covenant, the blood of bulls and goats served to purify the flesh – but not the conscience. Under the New Covenant, which came into full effect with the death and resurrection of Jesus, the conscience (part of the spiritual essence of man which is invisible to the naked eye) is purged and cleansed from dead works – prepared to serve the living God.

A testament is a form of last will, expressing the wishes and disposition of one's property after the testator's death. Webster's dictionary also defines testament as a covenant between God and the human race. Jesus' life, death, and resurrection – His defeat of the powers of darkness during his three day burial period, -- these acts fulfilled the universal legal requirements set by God Himself. Long ago, God set the shedding of blood as the requisite for the remission of sin. (Hebrews 9:22)

But the blood of bulls and goats could not suffice for this monumental act of remission. The blood of a pure man was the only remedy for the craven condition of mankind. Because God loved His created mankind so much, He wrapped a portion of Himself in flesh. This Son of man and Son of God lived a perfect life following His holy birth. Then as a representative of the entire human race, He took on all the sin of mankind, throughout the ages. He took all the punishment and curses due mankind, upon Himself. He nailed the Old Covenant of sin and death to the cross (Colossians 2:14). He bore it all – thereby paying the price for the remission of sins and the redemption of mankind into God's favor once again. Oh, what a selfless act! Oh, what an act of love!

On the great day of atonement described in Leviticus 16:1-22, the high priest made atonement for the sanctuary, the priests, and the people. The high priest would take off all his official ornaments and first offer a sin offering for himself and for the priesthood. He would enter the inner sanctum, the Holy of Holies, with the blood. He sprinkled the blood on the Mercy Seat. Afterward he sacrificed two male goats for the nation – one was killed for Jehovah. The other bore all the sins of the people. That scapegoat was taken outside the city and released into the wilderness.

Under the first covenant, sin was "covered", not erased. Under the New Covenant, sins were not "covered".

Sins were "put away" (Kenyon, 1999,p. 37) or remitted. With remission our sins are wiped out, as if they never existed. Now, committing sin breaks our fellowship with the Father; however, it does not break our relationship. (If we commit sins after our rebirth, our sins can be forgiven through confession and the intercession of Jesus Christ.)

I John 1:9 states: **"If we confess our sins, he is faithful and just to forgive us our sins, and to cleanse us from all unrighteousness."**

You have heard me speak in almost every reflection about you being the Righteousness of God. I have also spoken about the need to rid yourself of sin- consciousness and guilt by believing that you are the Righteousness of God.

Today the Holy Spirit has led me to go into detail about what Jesus has done for us through His finished work on earth. I must give credit to E.W. Kenyon and his great book, ***New Creation Realities***. It helped me to break down the complexities of redemption that might be otherwise missed or misunderstood. I want to share these insights with you.

We all know the Bible stories of Jesus' life and death in this earthly realm. As readers and students of His Word, we are familiar with most aspects of Jesus' earthly journey. But do we truly understand what Jesus did for us in His life, death, and resurrection? Often Christians proclaim that their sins have been forgiven and that they are new creatures in Christ – but do they really know the deepest meanings of Christ's redemptive work? When Jesus died, the veil in the temple was rent. (Matthew 27:51) This tearing of the veil leading into the Holy of Holies indicated an unveiling of the secrets of God's Word.

CHAPTER 1

THE LAW IS DEAD

Let me start with the most controversial portion of my treatise. The remainder will be essays in support of the controversy – to explain more fully the back story for these foregone conclusions.

Romans 7 in the King James Version of the Bible, relates part of Paul's letter to the Romans. Paul was not among the men who walked with Jesus while He was on this earth. However, Paul had a personal encounter with Jesus as he travelled to Damascus. (Acts 9:1-18) As a result of this divine encounter and Paul's extensive education in Jewish doctrine, Paul was chosen as the person to reveal the mysteries of God's plan to mankind.

Paul looked deeply into the recesses of the Old Covenant and the Law of Moses. He reviewed all in light of the gospel of Jesus Christ and the revelation knowledge granted to him from heaven. The result is the unfolding of the real meaning of Christianity and the finished work of Jesus Christ.

Jesus said: **"Suppose ye that I am come to give peace on earth? I tell you, Nay; but rather division:**

For from henceforth there shall be five in one house divided, three against two, and two against three." (Luke 12:51-52) The finished work of Jesus did not bring peace, but caused a division that lingers in the Church today. There are those who are attempting to practice Old Covenant religion in the guise of the New Covenant. Others are unapologetically stuck in the Old Covenant ways. A blessed few have peeped behind the veil into the Holy of Holies – and live under the Grace provided by the finished work of Jesus Christ.

"For the woman which hath an husband is bound by the law to her husband so long as he liveth; but if the husband be dead, she is loosed from the law of her husband. So then if, while her husband liveth, she be married to another man, she shall be called an adulteress: but if her husband be dead, she is free from that law; so that she is no adulteress, though she be married to another man. Wherefore, my brethren, ye also are become dead to the law by the body of Christ; that ye should be married to another, even to him who is raised from the dead, that we should bring forth fruit unto God." (Romans 7:2-4)

Here Paul is really making an analogy. He is comparing the Jewish marriage laws to the state of new Christian converts. These new converts (or new creatures as we shall name them later in this book) no longer owe allegiance to the law (the ancient Mosaic law of the Jewish religion). The old covenant was under the Law of Sin and Death. That "husband" (the Old Covenant) was now dead. That marriage was now dissolved. Jesus

Christ brought mankind a new covenant, straight from the Father. New Christian converts live under the Law of the Spirit of Life in Christ Jesus – a new marriage, a new covenant, purchased with the blood of Jesus.

The Law of Sin and Death emphasized all the rules, do's and don'ts of the Old Testament. Man's mind was constantly on sin – thus sin-consciousness. Man was ruled by fear and guilt. The Law had its purpose, -- to point out and identify sin. However, the Law did not have the power to keep one from sinning.

Under the new covenant, the new creature has the Holy Spirit. Jesus took the sin, guilt, fear, and condemnation upon Himself. In exchange He gave mankind His Righteousness. Jesus took the burden and gave mankind (all those who accept Him as Lord and Saviour) liberty. We call that gift GRACE.

Christians today choose either to live under fear and guilt, or under Grace. Many live a life of confusion, trying to navigate both. The choice is often an unconscious one based on tradition. Grace is a conscious choice for those willing to study the Word of God and meditate on it. Hopefully, this book will assist in that process for those who have not already been prompted by the Holy Spirit to dig deeper.

God did not send His Son to earth to make our lives more difficult. Jesus brought us the gift of Grace. It is up to each individual Christian to believe and to receive this gift. As with all of God's gifts, nothing is forced. All is free will.

Many define Grace as undeserved favor. Yes, we may feel we don't deserve the gift Jesus is offering us. We may feel we don't deserve to walk around the earth guilt-free and fear-free. But God wanted us to have the opportunity to do so. I cannot argue with the Father. Father knows best!

It was and is impossible to live sin-free under the Law. It is not impossible to live sin-free under the new covenant confirmed by Jesus Christ. He sent a Comforter, an Assistant to help us. Thank God for the Holy Spirit!`

CHAPTER 2

THE SHAME OF IT ALL

It is a shame that the message in this book has not been sufficiently realized and taught in our churches. Is this because of a lack of knowledge within the clergy – or is it a purposeful omission? Do shepherds purposefully withhold the truth to keep the sheep unaware? God forbid. Do they withhold the truth to keep members paying tithes and offerings? Are Christians operating in a futile attempt to buy salvation and prosperity? God forbid! Tithing is not wrong, but the efficacy of tithing is driven by one's underlying motive for tithing.

I sincerely pity any shepherd who is holding back the spiritual progress of the Body of Christ for carnal purposes. His/her soul is in danger of hell fire. Through Ezekiel God warned false prophets: **"And will ye pollute me among my people for handfuls of barley and for pieces of bread, to slay the souls that should not die, and to save the souls alive that should not live by your lying to my people that hear your lies?**

Because with lies ye have made the heart of the righteous sad, whom I have not made sad; and strengthened the hands of the wicked, that he should not return from his wicked way, by promising him life.

…I will deliver my people out of your hand: and ye shall know that I am theLord." (Ezekiet 13:19, 22-23) Lying can take the form of commission or omission. To hold back vital revelation from the congregation is sinful, if the shepherd is aware of deeper truths -- deeper truths that might enlighten the Body and ease the burdens many Christians carry unnecessarily.

In Ezekiel 34: 2,4 God condemns the shepherds who feed themselves and not the flock. He condemns them for not strengthening the diseased, healing the sick, binding up what was broken, nor rescuing those driven away. How does this apply to the church today, Sister Jannah?

If, indeed, this message of the reality of redemption has been purposefully hidden or withheld to keep God's flock in ignorance and spiritual bondage – this is a grave sin. God forbid!

Shepherding is a serious assignment and a great responsibility. The shepherd is not only responsible for his/her soul –but for the souls of the flock in the shepherd's care. The good of the sheep should be the shepherd's priority. The feeding, growth, development and protection of a healthy flock are mandated.

Even the loss of one sheep is serious, and mandates leaving the ninety-nine present sheep to search for and recover that one lost. At least that is what Jesus says in

Luke 15: 3-6: **"What man of you, having an hundred sheep, if he lose one of them, doth not leave the ninety and nine in the wilderness, and go after that which is lost, until he find it?**

And when he hath found it, he layeth it on his shoulders rejoicing."

If Jesus was this concerned about one percent of his flock being lost – how much more should today's ministers be wailing at the backslider rates in their congregations! How many of the 300, or the 3,000 people who came to Christ this year at your church – how many of them are still with you and active in the Church? I'm sure the retention rate is low, low, low. In fact, some of those still sitting on pews every Sunday, are living like sinners or ready to fly the coup. But today's pastors seem oblivious to this low retention rate. They feel like they've done their jobs when the person comes up front to the altar, says the prayer of salvation, and gets baptized. Unfortunately, after that the new believer is often on his/her own.

Most newly converted Christians follow a similar pathway into and out of Christianity. The pastors and or relatives tend to beat them over the head with erroneous Christian dogma – when the poor lamb doesn't even know the Bible stories they proudly expound. They do this instead of enticing the new member, the lamb, with Christian truths. The first lessons, sermons, and counsel they receive simply heighten their sin-consciousness and guilt. The teachings emphasize defeat instead of the present victory. The new converts are shamed and brow-beaten into positions of submission that glorify the "teacher" – not the Lord Jesus and His finished work.

The lambs are not given a clear understanding of what accepting Jesus Christ as Lord and Savior really means. The discourse they hear brings out an emotional response that is void of real understanding. No, not sense-knowledge, but spiritual understanding. They don't know and are not taught the reality of redemption – what it really means to be "saved" (what they are being "saved" from and to). I would guesstimate that 75% of new Christians cannot articulate the meaning of their "salvation". One reason is that the meaning is not explained. The other reason is that their mentors, themselves, do not know the real meaning of salvation.

Redemption is more than an exercise to satisfy the physical requirements outlined in the scripture – confessing Jesus as Lord and Savior; being baptized; and receiving the gift of the Holy Spirit. A new believer can do all of these and basically still be confused. The new believer has done what he/she hopes will ease the pain and guilt of their heretofore sinful lives, but they don't know what to do next – and they don't know what this all means. Unfortunately neither do many of their teachers/leaders.

Most churches are not set up to answer the questions and doubt that confront the new member. Some lambs have a brief two-hour New Member Class. Others have a more prolonged and comprehensive eleven-week New Member Class.

Having experienced the eleven-week class myself, I can tell you that one day a week for eleven weeks does not prepare you for the Christian walk. You feel more confident when you graduate, but you are not ready for the spiritual fight set before you. Your armour may have been ordered, but believe me, it has not yet been delivered.

Most churches today are not set up to nurture the new members, the lambs of the flock. Jesus would be appalled at the neglect of the lambs and the arrogance of the shepherds. Note that Jesus spent three years with His disciples (His flock) before they approached readiness to survive without His physical presence.

In this book I hope to bring more clarity to redemption. The redemption process is simple, but its deeper meaning is more complex. The finished work of Jesus Christ provided all of the heavy lifting in the redemptive process – remission of all sin, removal of a dead spirit, installation of God's nature of love within, and a roadmap for renewal of the mind. Renewal of the mind brings reconciliation of the human (sense-driven, carnal) mind with the Spirit of God which is now resident within the new creation man or woman. The ultimate goal of mind renewal is leadership and rulership by the Spirit within the new creation man/woman. The new creature is no longer a slave to the senses and carnal self, but walks by the Spirit of God.

"Therefore if any man be in Christ, he is a new creature: old things are passed away; behold, all things are become new." (2 Corinthians 5:17)

"For as many as are led by the Spirit of God, they are the sons of God." (Romans 8:14)

"(For we walk by faith, not by sight:)" (2 Corinthians 5:7)

Rulership by the Spirit engenders power and abilities that the new creation man has never even imagined. With the Spirit of God living inside him, the new creation man has become the Righteousness of God. The new creation man/woman receives God's wisdom, sanctification, and Eternal Life. What a benefits package!

But most new Christians are never educated about the benefits of redemption. They continue to practice the "Old Testament religion" taught by their mentors – using the Ten Commandments and irrelevant ordinances as their spiritual compass. This compass is companion to a giant dose of sin-consciousness. To educate means "to lead out". Most new Christians are never led out of "the old ways" lodged within the Law of Sin and Death.

The new Christian needs to be purposely taught about the Old Covenant and the New Covenant – the Law of Sin and Death vs the Law of the Spirit of Life in Christ Jesus. **"For the law of the Spirit of life in Christ Jesus hath made us free from the law of sin and death."** (Romans 8:2) Current introductions to Christianity tend to promote a new and different bondage, sin-consciousness.

Following chapters will further explain the Old and New Covenants and the reconciliation assignment that each new Christian should receive with full knowledge and understanding. The goal of the shepherd is to move the sheep to a point where each is actively involved in the ministry of reconciliation – on a personal level, while encouraging their peers in this Godly effort as well.

I pray that my Almighty Father in Heaven will give me the strength, insight, courage, revelation, and inspiration needed to organize these chapters into a coherent message that will bless every reader with a deeper understanding of the reality of redemption. In Jesus' Name. Amen.

"That it might be fulfilled which was spoken by the prophet, saying I will openmy mouth in parables, I will utter things which have been kept secret from the foundation of the world." (Matthew 13:35)

Brothers, Sisters get ready to receive a spiritual awakening that will remove scales from your eyes, as they fell from the eyes of Saul when he received the revelation of the reality of redemption.

CHAPTER 3

THE STAGES OF REDEMPTION

Actually there are no stages to redemption. Redemption is accomplished in one fell swoop by a man or woman accepting Jesus Christ as his/her Savior and confessing Jesus Christ as Lord. Immediately that man or woman is redeemed. Immediately that old dead spirit within man is replaced by the Nature of God.

That man may not look different on the outside, but a radical change has taken place in the inner man.

The work of Jesus is finished for all time. However, the work of the newly converted man is not finished. It has only just begun. The new convert does not become an "instant saint" although remission of sins is immediately guaranteed. The new convert is sin-free. The new convert is the Righteousness of God through the Grace of God and the faith of Jesus Christ. The convert is a New Creation, a new species of man – a man with God's Nature living inside him. The new convert immediately attains Eternal Life.

Ephesians 2:1-9 sums it up: **"And you hath he quickened, who were dead to trespasses and sins;**

Wherein in time past ye walked according to the course of this world, according to the prince of the power of the air, the spirit that now worketh in the children of disobedience:

Among whom also we all had our conversation in times past in the lusts of our flesh, fulfilling the desires of the flesh and of the mind; and were by nature the children of wrath, even as others.

But God, who is rich in mercy, for his great love wherewith he loved us, Even when we were dead in sins, hath quickened us together with Christ, (by grace ye are saved;)

And hath raised us up together, and made us sit together in heavenly places in Christ Jesus:

That in ages to come he might show the exceeding riches of his grace in his kindness toward us through Christ Jesus.

For by grace are ye saved through faith, and that not of yourselves: it is the gift of God.

Not of works, lest any man should boast."

We are saved by Grace through the unflinching faith of Jesus Christ. Our spirits were dead (due to sin and trespasses). Man could not meet the demands of the Mosaic Law. It was an impossible feat for a man with a dead spirit. But Jesus changed it all by His blood sacrifice. He became our eternal High Priest who knew no sin. His blood sacrifice covered all mankind – Jew and Gentile. He delivered mankind from the powers of satan – the powers of darkness, the powers of sin and death. He replaced our sin with His Righteousness. He replaced death with Eternal Life. Man does not receive these gifts until he accepts Jesus Christ as Savior and confesses the Lordship of Jesus Christ. It's that simple. The Father did not make it hard to receive salvation. Man has complicated the process with man-made superfluities.

According to Kenyon, (2011, p.66) *"Sin-consciousness has robbed us in the past of our faith, robbed us of our sense of worthiness, and robbed us of our joy. We were complete in Christ, but we did not know it (or believe it). That's how satan keeps us in darkness and weakness."*

Brothers and sisters, you are complete in Christ.

CHAPTER 4

RIGHTEOUSNESS VS SIN-CONSCIOUSNESS

What is Righteousness? According to 2 Corinthians 5:21: **"For he hath made him to be sin for us, who knew no sin; that we might be made the righteousness of God in him."** (KJV) The Amplified translates that verse as follows: **"For our sake He made Christ [virtually] to be sin Who knew no sin, so that in and through Him we might become [endued with, viewed as being in, and examples of] the righteousness of God [what we ought to be, approved and acceptable and in right relationship with Him, by His goodness].** In the next verse, 2 Corinthians 6:1 (AMP) Paul urges us not to receive this gift and then not use it: **"Laboring together [as God's fellow workers] with Him then, we beg of you not to receive the grace of God in vain [that merciful kindness by which God exerts His holy influence on souls and turns them to Christ, keeping and strengthening them – do not receive it to no purpose].**

Righteousness is a gift from God. Righteousness is *"the ability to stand in the Father's presence without the sense of guilt or inferiority, when we know that we have as good a standing before the Father as Jesus had in His earth walk, then theproblem of faith is settled."* (Kenyon, 2011, p. 102)

This state of being, this state of Righteousness is not some pie in the sky, fantasy- borne, high hope. This state was purchased for each and every child of God, by the blood of Jesus Christ. Jesus took on our sins and transgressions and gave us His Righteousness. Seems an unfair trade or substitution – but that's how much He loves us. And the gift just keeps on giving – in perpetuity for all mankind, -- yesterday, today, and for ever. The realization of the reality of your Righteousness is the key to accessing or appropriating all that God has given you as a born-again Christian. Yes, you may still make mistakes as you work on renewing your mind. But those mistakes can be forgiven, covered under the blood. Just repent and God will forgive under our New Covenant. According to John 1 1:9 KJV : **"If we confess our sins, he is faithful and just to forgive us our sins, and to cleanse us from all unrighteousness."**

This is a reality of redemption that each Christian must accept and live by in order to be a conduit for the power of Almighty God. And the blessing/gift is fourfold. I Corinthians 1;30 KJV states: **"But of him are ye in Christ Jesus, who of God is made unto us wisdom, and righteousness, and sanctification, and redemption."** You are redeemed! You are sanctified! You are the Righteousness of God! You have wisdom! Let's look at the Amplified version of this particular verse, I Corinthians 1:30 (AMP): **"But it is from Him that** you have your life in Christ Jesus, Whom God made our Wisdom from God, [revealed to us a knowledge of the divine plan of salvation previously hidden, manifesting itself as] our Righteousness [thus making us upright and putting us in right standing with God], and our Consecration [making us pure and holy], and our Redemption [providing our ransom from eternal penalty of sin]."

Whoa!! And it is not of works, but it is all a gift from God to mankind, to His New Creation, certified by the finished work of Jesus Christ of Nazareth.

These are spiritual things, which are taught by the Holy Spirit. They are foolishness to the natural man. These things are spiritually discerned. Your spirit recognizes the truth in this lesson. I Corinthians 2:12 confirms: **"Now we have received, not the spirit of the world, but the spirit which is of God; that we might know the things that are freely given to us of God."** God has freely given us redemption, consecration/sanctification (purity and holiness), righteousness and wisdom. All we have to do is believe His Word. The work is done. The price has been paid.

If you were to win the state lottery, it would not profit you to stand in your living room saying, "I don't believe that I really won" over and over. You would be just as poor financially as someone who did not purchase a ticket. You have to accept your victory and claim your winnings. Likewise with your divine inheritance, you must claim your victory. You must follow the process to renew your mind and reconcile the fellowship between your mind and spirit, until your spirit takes full control of your thinking and your actions.

It may not **feel** like your victory, because Jesus did all of the heavy lifting. But realize that Jesus Christ is the head, and you are part of His body, the Church. The head does nothing without the body. Many times Paul and others compared the relationship between Jesus and the Church as one between the Head and the Body. We were crucified with Jesus – Galatians 2:20.

Jesus bore all the punishments due mankind, and mankind is able to reap all of the benefits and promises due to the children of God. It's hard to conceive, because Jesus' actions were such an act of love and selflessness. We cannot imagine ourselves doing such a selfless act. But His ways and thoughts are high above ours. (Isaiah 55:9) God operates universally. We operate in the small space of our finite lives, often denying the ability we have as joint heirs with Jesus Christ.

Sisters and brothers, please accept your inheritance. Please acknowledge the veracity of your victory in Christ. Satan has used sin-consciousness and our struggle to live in the Old Covenant ways, even though we have been freed by the New Covenant. Sin-consciousness causes us to doubt because we feel as if we are unworthy of God's blessings. This is how satan keeps us weak and in darkness. He constantly accuses us. (Revelations 12:10) You must realize that you have the victory over satan and his cohorts, because Jesus (a human with God's nature inside him) defeated satan and the kingdom of darkness on our behalf over 2000 years ago. Jesus was the first-born among the new species of man. According to Romans 8:29 KJV : **"For whom he did foreknow, he also did predestinate to be conformed to the image of his Son, that he might be the firstborn among many brethren."** Jesus is our big brother. We are all sons and daughters of God. We are in God's family with the same rights, privileges and abilities that Jesus had. Until we realize and believe this, we will act as ineffectual wimps in the face of this world's many problems. Once we accept the reality of who we are – we become powerful tools of God! Hallelujah!!

Because I cannot say it any better, I am going to directly quote from pages 103 and 104 of Kenyon's *New Creation Realities* (2011).

"Now Jesus is made unto us Wisdom.

Every believer ought to know that, just as they know they have an umbrella or a raincoat during the rainy season, and before they start out, they put on their rubbers, don their raincoats, and take their umbrella and go to the office.

When you go out in the morning to face life's hard problems, you should remember these facts:

You have His Wisdom now to meet every need of today.

You have to meet a number of people. Some of them are going to be very difficult, but you have His wisdom and His Ability to make the contacts and go through the business successfully.

You have Wisdom superior to theirs. They have nothing but material, human wisdom. You have His Wisdom.

He has been made unto you Wisdom.

Not only that, but you are His Righteousness. That gives you access to the Throne at any time.

You can stand in His presence just as Jesus did in His earth walk, because Jesus is your Righteousness.

There can be no event so great but what His Wisdom and His Righteousness will enable you to meet it successfully.

You see, when you become the Righteousness of God, that really makes you a Master of Circumstances.

That lets you into the Inner Circle.

That gives you the advantage of the Father's Wisdom and Ability to put you over.

Satan cannot cope with the man who knows he is the Righteousness of God in Christ, who knows that Jesus has been made unto him Wisdom.

That man is a Master man.

You see, that leads you into the Superman Realm. Take accounts of stock for a moment.

You have God's very Nature in you.

The old life that kept you in bondage has stopped being.

The old self that was dominated by circumstance and by satan has stopped being, and a New Self, a dominant Self, a Righteous Self, a God-filled Self has taken its place.

You now have a legal right to the use of Jesus' Name.

Before the Master ascended, you remember He said in Matthew 28:18, "All authority has been given unto me in heaven and on earth." That authority is for the Members of the Body. Jesus doesn't need it.

He and the Father are one, so all that the Father is , Jesus is. This authority was given to the Church.

The ability to use that authority is given to us in the Holy Spirit.

We not only have this authority, but we have the great Mighty Spirit who raised Jesus from the dead dwelling in us, and when He came into us, He brought all His Ability, the Ability that he exercised in the resurrection of the Master, the Ability that He exercised in Christ. It is all in Him.

No wonder John said by the Spirit, in John 4:4, 'Greater is he that is in you than he that is in the world.'

You see, we are dominant people. We have the creative Ability of God in us. No limit to where we can go."

Sin-consciousness is the devil's tool to cause us to focus on the priorities of the Old Covenant. Sin-consciousness focuses on magnifying our mistakes and our trespasses. Sin-consciousness causes righteousness, sanctification, wisdom, and redemption to appear far away; and to appear as goals which the born-again Christian must **earn**. Sin-consciousness tells the born-again Christian that he/she has deficits that he/she must remedy by works. Sin-consciousness is a result of the devil's biggest and most successful lie. **The lie: You don't already have redemption, righteousness, sanctification,wisdom, and power through the Holy Spirit – you should fear satan's power and ability.** Until the Christian questions and fully dismisses the big lie as falsehood – he/she cannot fully live in the realm of the New Covenant; under the Law of the Spirit of Life in Christ Jesus.

Sin-consciousness is the product of a carnal mind, held captive in the sense realm. The carnal mind cannot understand or accept spiritual revelation because the sense-mind is in charge. The new nature of the newly created man must gain ascendency (or control) in the Christian's life through renewal of the mind. Renewal of the mind – of that sense-fed and sense-developed carnal mind, can only be accomplished by the washing of water by the Word of God. (Ephesians 5:26)

Sister Jannah, this seems far out and difficult. Listen, that is also a deception of satan. Immersing your mind in the Word is actually a pleasant task. It only seems hard because the sense-controlled mind does not want to submit to the Nature of God inside the born-again Christian. Immersion in the Word is like taking a walk through the Garden of Eden – joy, peace, and revelation.

The born-again Christian must realize that the devil is a liar and the father of lies. (John 8:44) Jesus has already purchased our redemption from satan's pawn shop. We already have wisdom, redemption, righteousness, and sanctification. We do not lack in any of these areas. Satan's insistence that we don't possess these gifts is the big lie. We are not just "sinners saved by grace". We are the Righteousness of God in Jesus Christ.

If a kidnapper is paid the amount owed to retrieve the kidnapped person, the kidnapper no longer has any right to hold the kidnapped person hostage. But if the kidnapped person will not willingly leave captivity, what is the ransom-payer to do? If the freed kidnap victim does not acknowledge his/her free state, he/she might willingly remain a captive forever – never having the courage to trust the ransom and walk out of the gates of captivity.

Brothers and sisters, Jesus has paid the price. Boldly walk out of your imagined captivity into your inheritance. God has your back. The finished work of Jesus and the Word of God reinforce and meet the legal requirements for your release.

CHAPTER 5

SUBSTITUTION

First, we need to understand the concept of "substitution". Substitution in common, everyday language is the replacement of one thing or person with another. Webster's Third International Dictionary (1993) defines substitution as "the nomination of someone to be heir upon the failure of an heir to take the inheritance or on his death". Webster defines "substitute" as "a person who takes the place of or acts instead of another". The work of the Father, through His Son, Jesus, was grounded in substitution. Our redemption is grounded in substitution.

Before Jesus' death and resurrection, man lived under the Old Covenant. The Old Covenant was the covenant of the Law. The Law came from the Ten Commandments and the many rules and regulations given to the children of Israel throughout the Old Testament. The people of God often tried to follow and obey all of the laws and regulations – but were by and large unsuccessful. There was a lot to remember and a great deal to live up to. If you broke one law, you might as well have broken them all. Sin was sin. If you broke one ordinance or disobeyed one law, you were a sinner – subject to all of the punishments or curses attached. It was hard!

You all know how hard it was because you **have lived** or **are still living** under the Law of Sin and Death – not because you have to, but because you have not yet realized the reality and entirety of what Jesus Christ did for you in His finished work. You are trying to obey the Ten Commandments and even some man-made rules with your own strength, instead of taking advantage of your salvation and the marvellous substitutions Jesus actualized on your behalf.

This is my prayer for myself and for each of you. Actually, this is the prayer of Paul for all Christians. Ephesians 1:15-22:

"Wherefore I also, after I heard of your faith in the Lord Jesus, and love unto all the saints,

Cease not to give thanks for you, making mention of you in my prayers,

That the God of our Lord Jesus Christ, the Father of glory, may give unto you the spirit of wisdom and revelation in the knowledge of him,

The eyes of your understanding being enlightened; that ye may know what is the hope of his calling, and what the riches of the glory of his inheritance in the saints,

And what is the exceeding greatness of his power to us-ward who believe, according to the working of his mighty power,

Which he wrought in Christ when he raised him from the dead, and set him at his own right hand in the heavenly places.

Far above all principality, and power, and might, and dominion, and every name that is named, not only in this world, but also in that which is to come.

And hath put all things under his feet, gave him to be the head over all things to the church,

Which is his body, the fulness of him that filleth all in all."

I have read these verses, with little understanding, many times. I have confessed these verses, with faith, in the past. Now God has provided the opportunity for understanding. No meditation on God's Word is fruitless. In due season, the Holy Spirit will open up the meaning, if you only believe and have patience. Ask for wisdom and you will receive. (James 1:5)

We need to first see, and then understand, what we are involved in. This is no small thing. This is a monumental topic to approach and wrap your head around. As with all spiritual accomplishments, it takes faith. I would advise confessing the above scriptures on a daily basis for a while. The revelation, understanding, and subsequent wisdom will come. Per Kenyon (2011), wisdom is the right use of knowledge. We want to use the wisdom generated by these scriptures to draw nearer to God and to activate the working of the Holy Spirit within. We want to generate the power within and direct it against interior and external obstacles, on behalf of ourselves, our families, our fellow Christians, our communities, and our world.

The whole world is waiting for the manifestation of the sons of God. We are those sons, and it's time to manifest the resurrection power within. (Romans 8:19)

That same power that resurrected Christ from the grave is in me and you. That resurrection power and ability is in us. (Romans 8:11) No weapon formed can prevail against us – we are undefeated and undefeatable. We just have to believe that and see ourselves through the prism of the blood of Jesus and His finished work.

What are you talking about Sister Jannah? Explain what you mean. O.K., I will.

As contradictory and impossible as it may seem to the carnal mind, Jesus Christ fully substituted Himself for you, me, all of the faithful who lived and died under the Mosaic law of sin and death, and all souls who are yet to be born again.

First know that each believer is born of God. John 3:5 says; **"Verily, verily, I say unto thee: Except a man be born of water and of the Spirit (born again), he cannot enter into the kingdom of God."**

Yes, in the physical world we make a confession of fealty (faithfulness) to Jesus Christ, ask for forgiveness of sins, are baptized in the water, and finally baptized with the

Holy Spirit (Holy Ghost). But there is an unseen spiritual change that occurs. We may not have had it explained to us at the time. **The reason is that this spiritual change is not realized and understood by many.**

Sisters and brothers, we do not belong to this earth. We are citizens of heaven. Jesus speaks of the disciples in John 17:16: **"They are not of the world, even as I am not of the world."**

We were specifically chosen by God. Per John 17:6: **"I have manifested thy name unto the men which thou gavest me out of the world: thine they were, and thou gavest them me; and they have kept thy word."**

So, **Fact #1** is: You did not choose Jesus. The Father chose you and gave you to Jesus.

Fact #2: Once Jesus defeated the powers of darkness in the underworld, He took all power in heaven and in earth. He defeated death and the grave. He holds the keys to death and hell. Jesus stripped the devil of all his authority.

During the hours and days following the crucifixion, Jesus was not merely lying in the tomb prepared for Him. He did battle with satan and his cohorts in the dark regions. Colossians 2:15 says: **"And having spoiled principalities and powers, he made a show of them openly, triumphing over them in it."**

In Revelations 1:18 Jesus says: **"I am he that liveth, and was dead; and behold, I am alive for evermore, Amen; and have the keys of hell and of death."**

Why did Jesus fight and win this battle? Hebrews 2:14b states: **"Forasmuch then, as the children (us humans) are partakers of flesh and blood, he (Jesus) also himself likewise took part of the same; that through death he might destroy him that had the power of death, that is, the devil."** Also verse 15 says: **"And deliver them who through fear of death were all their lifetime subject to bondage."** Jesus took on flesh and blood to show us that flesh and blood beings can defeat satan. Jesus secured the victory to take all power from satan and to deliver us from a fear of satan and of death.

The battle was really man's battle to fight. Men were the ones who had failed to obey the Father in the Garden of Eden. Men were the ones who were stiff-necked and idol-worshipping ingrates. Men were the outlaws. But the Father had a plan to redeem man from the impossible-to-keep law and from the grips of the adversary. He dressed His own son, Jesus Christ, in flesh and sent Him to earth to be a **substitute** for fallen humanity. Because He loved us so, God sent a part of Himself to be the propitiation for our sins and to redeem us from the Law of Sin and Death. Thus begins the substitutionary work of Jesus Christ.

The entire redemption plan was a legal operation. Man could not legally be freed from the Law of Sin and Death; from the throes of hell – without the shedding of blood. God set it up that way. For thousands of years, the Israelites had been killing doves, sheep, goats and bulls to offer blood for the cleansing of their sins.

Fact #3: As a born-again Christian you are part of the Body of Christ. Therefore you were part of this victory over the powers of darkness. The head does not fight without the body. The head does not die without the body dying. The head is not resurrected without the body also being resurrected. Jesus Christ is the head, and we, as members of the Church, are His body.

As redeemed Christians we were crucified with Christ. Galatians 2:20 says**: "I am crucified with Christ: nevertheless I live; yet not I, but Christ liveth in me: and the life which I now live in the flesh I live by the faith of the Son of God, who loved me and gave himself for me."**

Colossians 2:12-14 states: **"Buried with him in baptism, wherein also ye are risen with him through the faith of the operation of God, who hath raised him from the dead.**

And you, being dead in your sins and the uncircumcision of your flesh, hath he quickened together with him, having forgiven you all trespasses:

Blotting out the handwriting of ordinances that was against us, which was contrary to us, and took it out of the way, nailing it to his cross."

And we were raised with Christ. Ephesians 2:19-20 states: **"Even when we were dead in sins, hath quickened us together with Christ, (by grace ye are saved;)**

And hath raised us up together, and made us sit together in heavenly places in Christ Jesus.

The miracle and the mystery is this: Once we become part of the Body of Christ, we share in the death, burial, and resurrection of Jesus Christ. We join God's family as sons and daughters of God. Our duty now is to walk in Him (Jesus) as He lives in us. We are to be rooted, grounded, built up, and established in the faith. Faith is the key that opens the treasures of wisdom and knowledge given to us by the finished work of Jesus. Colossians 2:6-7 states: **"As ye have therefore received Christ Jesus the Lord, so walk ye in him:**

Rooted and built up in him, and stablished in the faith, as ye have been taught, abounding therein with thanksgiving."

Romans 8:10-11 tells us: **"And if Christ be in you, the body is dead because of sin; but the Spirit is life because of righteousness.**

But if the Spirit of him that raised up Jesus from the dead dwell in you, he that raised up Christ from the dead shall also quicken your mortal bodies by his Spirit that dwelleth in you."

E.W. Kenyon explains in *New Creation Realities* that God chose us. God gave each of us to Jesus. Jesus' life, death, and resurrection – His defeat of the powers of darkness freed us from the power of satan , from the captivity of sin, and from the fear of death.

We received remission of our sins. Do you understand remission? To remit means: to desist from an activity; to release from guilt or penalty; to refrain from exacting a penalty; to cancel or refrain from inflicting a penalty; to restore or consign to a former status or condition. Jesus' death brought something beyond forgiveness of sin. It stopped the activity of sin in our lives. It released us from guilt and from the penalty for our trespasses. It wiped out our sin as if it never existed. Jesus took all penalty upon Himself. These selfless acts of Jesus Christ restored us to our former condition, without the burden of sin. He freed us from the Law of Sin and Death. As it says in Colossians 2:14: **Blotting out the handwriting of ordinances that was against us, which was contrary to us, and took it out of the way, nailing it to his cross."** Mankind (you and I) now live under a New Covenant, the Law of the Spirit of Life in Christ Jesus. Jesus became our high priest, and His precious blood was substituted for all of the punishment that was due mankind. Jesus **legally** redeemed us.

CHAPTER 6

SUBSTITUTIONS IN THE NEW CREATION

As noted in the last chapter, man's ultimate redemption was accomplished through a number of substitutions. Most of the substitutions can be observed along the lines of belonging to the Old Covenant (grounded in Mosaic Law) or the New Covenant mediated by Jesus Christ.

The first substitution finds Jesus substituting Himself as the outlaw – in the place of mankind, and then bearing all of the punishment due to mankind throughout the ages – both under the Old Covenant and under the New Covenant and for all ages to come. This may take effort to comprehend, as this substitution reaches far into the past and far into the future, and is eternal. *Eternal* is a difficult concept for finite-minded man to even imagine. Accepting this concept requires your faith in God's Word and its ultimate truth. The more you renew your mind, the clearer it will become.

Jesus bore all of the pain and suffering that were due mankind throughout the ages. He bore it all in

His own body on the cross. He substituted Himself for fallen mankind and took the punishment and curses due to mankind. He did so willingly and on purpose to accomplish the release of mankind from the captivity of satan and satan's dark forces. He took our sin and substituted His Righteousness. He became sin for us and made us the Righteousness of God in Himself. What favor we have found in God's love!

"For he hath made him to be sin for us, who knew no sin, that we might be made the righteousness of God in him." (2 Corinthians 5:21)

The Old Covenant was governed by the Law of Sin and Death, based on the Mosaic law and the many ordinances in the Old Testament of the Bible. The New Covenant substituted the Law of the Spirit of Life in Christ Jesus. Under the Old Covenant mankind was spiritually dead and estranged from the Father due to the disobedience of Adam and Eve. Man thereby broke his *relationship* and his *fellowship* with God.

Under the New Covenant, the old man is replaced by a new creature, or a new creation (new species). This new species is a man with the Nature of God within Him. Per Kenyon, *"That old, fallen, sin-ruled self was displaced and the new Jesus self, the New Creation self, the Godlike self, that self that is made in the image of Christ, became our new self."* (Kenyon, 2011, p. 62) **"Therefore if any man be in Christ, he is a new creature: old things are passed away; behold, all things are become new."** (2 Corinthians 5:17)

"There is therefore now no condemnation to them which are in Christ Jesus, who walk not after the flesh [senses], but after the Spirit. For the law of the Spirit of Life in Christ Jesus hath made me free from the law of sin and death." (Romans 8:1)

The Law of Sin and Death governed spiritually dead men. The Law of the Spirit of Life in Christ Jesus governs the re-created new man, the new species of man. The Law of the Spirit of Life in Christ Jesus governs you, as a born-again Christian.

The two covenants are not interchangeable. New creatures can only thrive under the Law of the Spirit of Life in Christ Jesus. New creatures who attempt to live under the Law of Sin and Death will be unsuccessful and will miss out on all the blessings Jesus Christ intended for the new creation man. The Law of Sin and Death is now null and void, but too many born-again Christians are trying to live under its precepts, because they have not been taught the reality of redemption.

That is why these teachings and your acceptance of them are so important. Until you realize who you are in Christ Jesus, you will not be able to appropriate or access the blessings, and power, and glory associated with your resurrected, new creature self. You will continue to waddle in the mud of sin-consciousness, guilt, condemnation, worthlessness and bondage. Even though you have been born again into God's royal family, you cannot access the privileges of your kingship.

"For if by one man's offence death reigned by one; much more they which receive abundance of grace and of the gift of righteousness shall reign in life by one, Jesus Christ." (Romans 5:17)

"And hast made us unto our God kings and priests: and we shall reign on the earth." (Revelation 5:10)

Who reigns? Kings reign. Realize your royal status.

By His finished work Jesus substituted mankind's estrangement from God by giving men and women the opportunity to renew their relationship and fellowship with the Father – by becoming sons of God, just as Jesus was a Son of God.

By His finished work Jesus substituted mankind's ostracism from the Throne of Grace and gave mankind a new port-of-entry into the Kingdom of God, and God's Family.

By His finished work Jesus substituted Eternal Life for death, hopelessness and despair under the bondages of satan.

By His finished work Jesus substituted mankind's suffering, lost humanity, old fallen and sin-ruled state – for a kingly glory as children of the King of kings and joint heirs with Jesus Christ. Mankind was redeemed from the hand of the adversary.

The old laws of the ten commandments and the Old Testament were replaced with one overarching summation: **"A new commandment I give unto you. That ye love one another; even as I have loved you, that ye also love one another.**

By this shall all men know that ye are my disciples, if ye have love one to another." (John 13:34-35 KJV)

James calls this commandment the royal law. **"If ye fulfil the royal law according to the scripture, Thou shalt love thy neighbour as thyself, ye do well:…"** (James 2:8)

Do all these things really belong to us? Ephesians 1:3 says: **"Blessed be the God and Father of our Lord Jesus Christ, who hath blessed us with every spiritual blessing."** The inheritances that Jesus substituted for man's miserable worldly state were spiritual blessings – only recognizable and perceivable with a spiritual mindset. The carnal mind cannot see or comprehend things of the Spirit. (1 Corinthians 2:14)

Through the finished work of Jesus Christ we were given the capability of being born again, from God. The travail of Jesus constituted the birth pangs that made our new birth possible, as we are delivered from darkness into the kingdom of His dear Son. (Colossians 1:13)

"Verily, verily, I say unto thee, Except a man be born again, he cannot see the kingdom of God." (John 3:3) A man cannot see, let alone enter, the kingdom of God without a new birth as a re-created man. So Jesus paved the way, as the first of many brethren (Romans 8:29)

"But the natural, nonspiritual man does not accept or welcome or admit into his heart the gifts and teachings and revelations of the Spirit of God – for they are folly (meaningless nonsense) to him; and he is incapable of knowing them [of progressively recognizing, understanding and becoming better acquainted with them] because they are spiritually discerned and estimated and appreciated." (1 Corinthians 2:14 AMP)

CHAPTER 7

THE HOUSE OF GOD

Throughout the Bible we have historical accounts of God's desire for a house, a dwelling place here on earth.

In Exodus 25:8 God said: **"Let them make me a sanctuary; that I may dwell among them."** God gave specific requirements for the tabernacle and the materials to be used in its construction. The tabernacle was portable and went with the Israelites as they moved from place to place in the wilderness. In Exodus 29:44 God promised to sanctify the tabernacle and the altar therein. Moses called the tabernacle the Tabernacle of Congregation. Often, the glory of the Lord filled the tabernacle (Exodus 40:35). In the tabernacle Aaron could make offerings to atone for himself, his household, and the people. He would sprinkle the blood of sacrificed animals onto the mercy seat (Leviticus 16: 11, 14, 16).

In 2 Samuel 7: 5 God told Nathan to ask David**, "Shalt thou build me an house for me to dwell in?"** God said to Nathan, **"Whereas I have not dwelt in any house since the time that I brought up the children of Israel out of Egypt, even to this day, but have walked in**

a tent and in a tabernacle." (2 Samuel 7:6) God was not satisfied with a temporary abode. He wanted a permanent dwelling place – **"Why build ye not me an house of cedar?** (2 Samuel 7:7)

David did not have the opportunity to finish God's House, but his heartfelt desire was accepted by the Lord. Solomon said, **"And the Lord said unto David my father, Whereas it was in thine heart to build an house unto my name, thou didst well that it was in thine heart."** God counted David's sincere desire as a job well done. Solomon, David's son, was assigned the completion of God's House, the temple. (1 Kings 8:18)

Once built, Solomon questioned the Lord's wisdom in wanting a house on earth. **"But will God indeed dwell on the earth? Behold the heaven and heaven of heavens cannot contain thee? how much less this house that I have builded?"**

Jesus upheld the sanctity of the temple when He ran the moneychangers and those who sold doves out of the temple. He said to them, **"It is written, My house should be called the house of prayer, but ye have made it a den of thieves."**

Oh! How many today are misusing the House of God for fame, personal gain, and other ungodly endeavors. I believe God is not pleased with this misuse of His sanctuary.

But God foresaw the ignorance of men. He already had a plan and a remedy for the situation.

In Hebrews 8 Paul speaks of God's plan for a dwelling place. God raised up a new priesthood after the order of Melchisedec (Hebrews 7:12) The Jewish priests were originally out of the tribe of Levi. **Our** new High Priest sprang out of the tribe of Judah. Jesus was not made high priest **"after the law of a carnal commandment, but after the power of an endless life"** (Hebrews 12:16). The Levites were humans who had to offer atonement for their own sins, as well as those of the people. Eventually every Levite priest had to die and be replaced. Jesus, from the line of Judah, was without sin and lives eternally.

(If you remember, Melchisedec appeared after Abraham's slaughter of the kings. The story is recounted in Hebrews 7. Melchisedec was priest of the Most High God, without father, mother, or line of descent – with neither beginning of days nor end of life – **eternal**. Hebrews 7:2 calls him the King of righteousness, King of Salem, and King of Peace. Sounds a lot like Jesus! Many occurrences in the Old Testament foreshadow or predict/prophesy events that actually take place in the New Testament. Melchisedec foreshadowed the coming of Jesus Christ.)

According to Paul in Hebrews, the law made nothing perfect, but Jesus brought in a better hope (Hebrews 7:19). Our Almighty Father made Jesus a guarantor of a better covenant. **"For those priests were made without an oath by him that said unto him, The Lord sware and will not repent, thou art a priest for ever after the Order of Melchisedec:"** (Hebrews 7:21) Because Jesus is eternal, His priesthood is forever and unchangeable. So we move from the Law of Sin and Death to the Law of the Spirit of Life in Christ Jesus – from the Old Testament Covenant to the New Testament Covenant. Yet the matter of God's dwelling still needs clarification.

Where is God's House now? Is it in the many thousands of churches, temples, and synagogues located around the United States of America? Is it in the millions of worship places established around the world? Where can God dwell? What sanctuary is pure enough for Him to occupy?

In Jeremiah 31:33 God promises: **"But this shall be the covenant that I will make with the house of Israel; After those days saith the Lord, I will put my law [my Word] in their inward parts, and write it in their hearts; and will be their God and they shall be my people."** This promise was fulfilled after the finished work of Jesus.

Under the old covenant, Moses received the law on tablets of stone. Under the new covenant, God's law is inscribed inside the believer, written on the believer's heart. When a man or woman accepts Jesus Christ as Lord and Savior and is baptized, the old spirit of sin and death is evicted and the Spirit of God (the Nature of God) moves into the heart.

Jesus was a human man with the Spirit of God living within Him. Jesus' finished work created a new species of man – men and women with the Spirit of God living in them. Sister Jannah, you couldn't be right! I still have bad thoughts and I still do the wrong thing sometimes. How can I have God's Spirit living in me? Just because the Spirit has moved in does not mean you are perfect yet. Your spirit is new, but your **mind** is still tied to the flesh and the senses. The reports of your touch, smell, taste, hearing, and sight are the input you are used to and the input you have based your decisions on all your life. If any man be in Christ, he is a new creature – a new creation. He is a natural man with God's Spirit inside him. That man's next task is to reconcile (or bring into fellowship) his mind and his spirit.

This requires renewal of the mind. Romans 12:2 says: **"…be ye transformed bythe renewing of your mind."** How do you renew your mind? Through hearing, reading, studying, meditating and **living** the Word of God.

So where is God's dwelling? – *not just among men*, **but in men**. I Corinthians 3:16 says: **"Know ye not that ye are the temple of God, and that the Spirit of God dwelleth in you?"** I Corinthians 6:19-20 states**: "What? Know ye not that your body is the temple of the Holy Ghost which is in you, which ye have of God, and ye are not your own? For ye are bought with a price: therefore glorify God in your body, and in your spirit, which are God's."** Jesus' life, death, and resurrection paid the price for you.

As you read, study, and live the Word of God, you clean up and sanctify the temple. You bring your mind and body into fellowship to serve the Living God. The Spirit will eventually over-rule the body and the mind. As you develop spiritually, The Holy Spirit will eventually take control of your thoughts, your will, and your actions. That Spirit within you will give you a heart to know God.

Jeremiah 24:7 says: **"And I will give them an heart to know me, that I am theLord: and they shall be my people, and I will be their God:…"**

Revelations 21:3 says: **"Behold, the tabernacle of God is with men, and he will dwell with them, and they shall be his people, and God himself shall be with them, and be their God."**

To make it even clearer, the Bible states in 2 Corinthians 6:16**: "…for ye are the temple of the living God; as God hath said, I will dwell in them, and walk in them; and I will be their God, and they shall be my people."** God moves around this planet in His people. God does His work through His people.

Wherever we go, we bring the light and love of God into the atmosphere. Though we are not yet perfect, the Spirit of God shines through us and around us. As we continue to sanctify God's temple by renewing our minds – the greater things that Jesus prophesied will be manifested in our lives. God has a new house, purchased by the blood of Jesus – **and that house is you**. Glorify Him with that house.

When others see you coming, let them see God coming their way. (Not that you are God, but God is in you, and **greater is He that is in you than he that is in theworld.** I John 4:4) Let God work in you and through you everyday. In Jesus' Name. Amen.

CHAPTER 8

HE'S NOT DEAD, HE'S ALIVE IN YOU

God's desire is an army of this new species – men and women filled with God; which means filled with the Father, Son, and Holy Spirit. But for the sake of simplicity, let us say men and women who are filled with Jesus Christ – and who are fully aware of ***"Jesus-within-me"*** at all times and under all circumstances.

That is a difficult pose to hold with the human mind constantly chattering its two cents worth into the thought arena. However the Spirit is greater. And the Word of God is more powerful. The solution is to bathe our minds in the pool of the Word of God daily. Read, study, meditate and live the Word. The Word will do the work. We only need provide contact opportunities. The Word is that powerful! Hebrews 4:12 says: **"For the word of God is quick, powerful, and sharper than any twoedged sword, piercing even to the dividing of soul and spirit, and of the joints and marrow, and is a discerner of the thoughts and intents of the heart."**

The Word can clearly discern products of the mind vs products of the Spirit. The Word supports the eventual ascendancy of the Spirit as the ruler of our lives. The Word is the platform upon which our spiritual evolution is built. Our spiritual evolution is from sense-ruled [flesh-ruled] to Spirit-led lives. The Word is the solid foundation of our salvation. Before we are born again, our lives are totally ruled by our senses. Once born-again, we begin the change to a Spirit-led life.

With the finished work of Jesus – Christ is in you. Just as Jesus spoke: **"At that day ye shall know that I am in my Father, and ye in me, and I in you."** (John 14:20) This was God's master plan all along; to abide in man as man abides in Him. **"…but ye know him; for he dwelleth with you, and shall be in you."** (John 14:17) How does God abide in man? By His Word. **"In the beginning was the Word, and the Word was with God, and the Word was God."** (John 1:1)

But I thought you said the Spirit of God, the Nature of God, was in me. Yes, and the word of God is spirit. John 6:63 says: **"It is the spirit that quickeneth; the flesh profiteth nothing: the words that I speak unto you, they are spirit and they are life."** The entire Bible is God speaking unto us. Think spiritually, not carnally.

John 3:30 states: **"He must increase, but I must decrease."** These words of John the Baptist apply to every born-again Christian. When Jesus comes into his/her life, the flesh-supported carnal mind must decrease and yield to the new Spirit within. The Spirit within is nurtured and strengthened by a constant influx of God's Word. The more of the Word that you digest, the more powerful your inner being becomes. As the Word enters, the Spirit uses the Word to minister to us.

When the Spirit of God takes residence within a man/woman, it is like a newborn baby – requiring nurture and proper feeding until it grows into the fullness of its power. God wants that Word written on the tablets of our hearts and ready to be spoken in whatever circumstance we find ourselves. "It is written…" As the Word gains control, Jesus gains control over that carnal, nonspiritual mind which has ruled all our lives.

The 20th chapter of St. John reveals one of our problems. When Mary Magdalene went to the grave of Jesus Christ, on the first day of the week, it was still dark. The stone had been removed from before the sepulcher. Mary immediately ran to tell Simon Peter. Simon Peter and another disciple came to the tomb and found nothing but the burial clothes and the linen that covered Jesus' head at burial. The disciples then left and went home. Mary Magdalene stayed and wept. When she looked back into the sepulcher she saw two angels, one at the head and one at the feet of where Jesus' body had lain. The angels asked: **"Woman, why weepest thou?"** She answered: **"Because they have taken away my Lord, and I know not wherethey have laid him"** – because she sought for a dead Jesus.

John 20:14-17 recounts that Mary then turned around and a man said unto her, **"Woman, why weepest thou? Whom seekest thou?"** Mary thought this man was the gardener, and that perhaps he knew the location of Jesus' body. This man was not the gardener. This man was the risen Jesus Christ. Jesus called her name and Mary immediately answered: **"Rabboni, which is to say, Master."** She recognized Jesus' voice.

This is the problem. Mary Magdelene was looking for a dead Jesus. But Jesus was alive and standing right next to her. Too many Christians have approached salvation with the idea that Jesus is dead – that yes, He rose again from the gravebut then was transfigured into the heavens. But to us down here on earth, He is dead. **Wake up! He is alive inside you!**

I am here to tell you all. Jesus is alive and well in the earth. Jesus dwells in every born-again Christian -- every Christian who has confessed Jesus Christ as Lord and Savior. The problem is that Christians see Jesus as a dead entity. On Easter we celebrate His resurrection, but deep in our hearts, we feel that He has left us alone in this desolate place called the earth realm. We see none of the power and none of the miracles He performed, or that He promised that we would perform in His stead. (John 14:12) The Church is not without spot or blemish. We, individually, are not without spot or blemish. We don't realize or understand our own worth and our own place in this spiritual landscape. We feel this way because we are looking for Jesus outside ourselves. But Jesus is alive and inside each born-again Christian. Each Christian must believe and acknowledge His presence within.

Until you see the reality of redemption. Until you recognize that as a born-again Christian, you are the temple of the Living God – you cannot know who you are and what you are. As long as you hold on to Old Testament mores, feeling that earthly high priests can atone for your sins, you are serving a dead savior. Jesus has already remitted all of your past sins and is willing to forgive any current trespasses, if you confess and ask for forgiveness. Your slate is clean. (1 John 1:9)

You are the Righteousness of God. You are sanctified for God's service. You have access to God's Wisdom. You are fully redeemed – without spot or blemish. But to BE this person, you have to realize, believe, and accept your pure state as you stand in Christ Jesus, and He stands inside of you. We need to stand up and act like our big brother, Jesus Christ.

The moment we believe in and accept Jesus, we become the Righteousness of God. We have been going before God with a sense of inferiority, rather than a sense of entitlement. We let the devil whisper our inferiority into our ears and then we grovel before the throne. Instead of going boldly to the throne, with confidence in our righteous state – we cast doubt immediately before the Throne of Grace, and then expect a good outcome. You cannot doubt your worthiness in your heart.

You have to KNOW who you are. You have to KNOW you are a child of God, not just any old bystander. You have to KNOW you have a well-established spiritual link to the Father and are part of the Family of God, not a stranger.

There are now only two commandments to follow: **"And thou shalt love the Lord thy God with all thy heart, and with all thy soul, and with all thy mind, and with all thy strength: this is the first commandment.**

And the second is like, namely this, Thou shalt love thy neighbor as thyself. There is none other commandment greater than these." (Mark 12:30-31)

"God's righteousness makes you fearless in Satan's presence." (Kenyon, 1999,p. 53) We are no longer weaklings, but stand before satan as Sons of God. What a difference that stance makes! Jesus never cowered in the presence of satan. He merely spoke the Word of God – "It is written". Satan had to flee. Jesus commanded and demons had to flee. Jesus spoke healing, and the sick were immediately healed. We have that same power. Jesus lives in us and we can speak the Word and overcome all the powers of satan.

"Behold, I give unto you power to tread on serpents and scorpions, and over all the power of the enemy: and nothing shall by any means hurt you." (Luke10:19)

Kenyon regrets that us men and women with God in them, are walking about the earth as **"mere men"** (Kenyon, 2011, p 124) We live in this state because we have not **developed** the recreated inner man [new creature, new creation]. Kenyon puts it this way:

"You see, the believer, when born into the Family, has a measure of Faith, has a measure of Love; the Love of God is shed abroad in his heart by the Holy Spirit. But unless he grows in Grace and in the knowledge of the Lord Jesus Christ, unless he studies to show himself approved unto the Father, ***he remains unspiritual***. *His spirit is never cultivated, never developed. You can develop your spirit as you can develop your mind, as you can develop your physical muscles.*

The average believer has never developed his spirit. Consequently his Faith is weak, his Love is weak, and his Knowledge is often mixed with error. You must remember that Love does not come from the reasoning faculties; neither does Faith. Faith and love are both born in the Recreated human spirit. The reason *Jesus said in Matt. 4:4 **"Man shall not live by bread alone, but by every word that proceedeth out of the mouth of God,"** was not to cultivate man's intellectual and reasoning faculties, but to cultivate his spirit....As long as we walk in the senses [flesh,carnal] and follow the inclinations of the senses [flesh, carnal], the spirit is not developed and we are walking as mere men."* (Kenyon, 2011, pp.124-125)

Per 2 Corinthians 3:6 : **"...Who also hath made us able ministers of the new testament:..."** Our ministry is reconciliation. We must first reconcile our individual minds with the Spirit of God within us. The Spirit within must dominate our thoughts and behavior. Then we must help fellow Christians to realize and reconcile their minds with the Spirit within.

The Spirit of God within us, the Nature of God within us – is love. If we love God and we love our fellow man as ourselves, no other commandments are necessary. All is covered. We just have to realize and accept the New Covenant, the new creation that we are, our new High Priest, and our new Ministry of Reconciliation. We have to give up the guilt-trek and sin-conciousness. It has been a comfortable rut for most of our lives – but the time is up for waddling in the mud of sin and death. Jesus' finished work delivered us from the pig pen of satan. We are part of God's Family now. We are spiritual royalty. We are no longer mere men. We need to act like it.

Mere men are carnal minded and ruled by the flesh (the senses). **"For they that are after the flesh [senses, carnal] do mind the things of the flesh [senses, carnal], but they that are after the Spirit the things of the Spirit.**

For to be carnally minded is death; but to be spiritually minded is life and peace.

Because the carnal mind is enmity against God: for it is not subject to the law of God, neither indeed can be.

So then they that are in the flesh cannot please God." (Romans 8:5-8)

To remain carnal, while knowing there is an escape from that narrow-mindedness, is pitiable. Christians need to pick up their crosses and follow Jesus' example.

Yes, it is work to throw off the old ways and pursue the new. It will sound crazy to your Christian family, friends, and church members. But you can't let that stop you. They may consider you arrogant when you proclaim, "I am the righteousness of God. I am sanctified. I have the wisdom of God. I am a son of God. I am a child of God." So be it! They balked when Jesus said that he was the Son of God. Yet it was true.

Man was a spiritual being in Eden. He became a carnal/flesh/sense being when he disobeyed his heavenly Father. Jesus paid the price for man to have the option to return to the Father as part of the Father's Family – sins fully remitted. Why wouldn't a man seek that reconciliation with the Father? Only because he does not understand that he has that option, and what choosing that option means. Father God, we thank you for the opportunity to understand and accept the redemptive work of our brother, Jesus Christ of Nazareth.

Pray: **Help us Father to walk that bridge between the two covenants by studying, meditating, and living Your Word. The Word is the key to full salvation and acceptance of our power as tools of God in this earth realm. When we realize and accept our redemption, God can take up full abode within our beings and work mighty works through us individually, and through His collective body, the Church. Help us to find and mobilize our new selves in Christ Jesus.**

Jesus Christ is not dead. He is alive in each born again Christian. Each of us must take on the ministry of reconciliation within, and then help others in the reconciliation process – that the bride may awaken and be prepared for the arrival of the bridegroom, without spot or blemish.

What does it mean – I am a new creation? A new creature? It means you have an opportunity set before you to knowingly mend your relationship with Father God and to become a valued Son of God. You understand that your dead spirit has vacated the premises. You have the opportunity to acknowledge that Jesus Christ lives within you and can work mightily through you.

Now you are a man or woman with God living inside. You are a new creation, a new creature, a new species of being. Jesus was the first of this new species.

"But of him are ye in Christ Jesus, who was made unto us wisdom from God, and righteousness and sanctification, and redemption." (1 Corinthians 1:30

Our new birth brings us these gifts. We need only to realize and accept the gifts to actualize them. If we don't know we have a tool in our possession, we cannot use the tool. If we do not realize we have the key – the door will remain locked and bar entrance into paradise.

CHAPTER 9

CHRIST IN YOU, THE HOPE OF GLORY

In our chapter on The House of God, it becomes evident that God has always desired to dwell with man, and ultimately in man. From the tabernacle to the temple, churches and synagogues – brick and mortar edifices -- to the inner man.

The whole point of redemption is to allow each of us to become an instrument of God's will. But participation is voluntary, as God never violates our free will.

To recap, Adam and Eve gave away their divine birthright – Eden and the abiding presence of God. They gave this away for Satan's deceptions. They pawned Eternal Life for a bite of forbidden fruit – sense knowledge. The Tree of the Knowledge of Good and Evil was just an introduction to living via the flesh or the senses, instead of living by the Spirit of God. It seemed like wisdom, but it was merely sense-knowledge and the sin-consciousness that comes with it. Jesus Christ gave His blood to purchase man's redemption from the prisons of satan and back into the Family of God.

Sometimes satan's prisons look like prosperity – fame, money, notoriety. Other times satan's prisons look like what they really are – drug addiction, evil soul ties, perversions of all sorts, misery, anguish, and pain. Regardless of the manifestation of man's spiritual imprisonment, no good can be the result, and the soul is captive. The spirit of that man or woman is dead, and only the power of God can replace it with a living spirit (God's Nature of Love) and Eternal life.

God's ultimate plan, once He looked into the future at man's creation, was a plan to legally bring man back to Himself, voluntarily. God immediately foresaw the flaws in man's design and worked out an intricate plan to remedy them – over centuries. That's why so many passages in the Old Testament predict the coming of Christ. God sees the end from the beginning.

"Remember the former things of old: for I am God, and there is none else; I am God, and there is none like me, **"Declaring the end from the beginning, and from ancient times the things that are not yet done, saying, My counsel shall stand, and I will do all my pleasure."** (Isaiah 46:9-10)

God designed a plan to ransom mankind from the bondage of satan. The ultimate goal of the plan is to result in a new species of man – a man with God living inside him. This is the new creature (the new creation) spoken of in 2 Corinthians 5:17. **"Therefore if any man be in Christ, he is a new creature: old things are passed away; behold, all things are become new."**

"And all things are of God, who hath reconciled us to himself, by Jesus Christ, and hath given to us the ministry of reconciliation.

To wit, that God was in Christ, reconciling the world unto himself, not imputing their trespasses unto them; and hath committed unto us the word of reconciliation." (2 Corinthians 5:17-19).

The ministry associated with the Old Covenant was the ministry of atonement – a mere covering of sin. The ministry of the New Covenant is **reconciliation**. Our new High Priest, Jesus Christ, **"...became us, who is holy undefiled, separate from sinners, and made higher than the heavens"** (Hebrews 7:26) Jesus Christ is **"...a minister of the sanctuary, and of the true tabernacle, which the Lord pitched, and not man."** (Hebrews 8:12) The first covenant had ordinances of divine service and a worldly sanctuary (Hebrews 9:11). Jesus came to take away the first covenant, that he might establish the second and better covenant – the Law of the Spirit of Life in Christ Jesus. The tabernacle which the Lord pitched is the new creation man.

Firstly, man must hold the beginning of his confidence steadfast until the end. The clarification provided by the Pauline doctrine (the writings of Paul) cannot be dismissed in favor of the Old Covenant teachings (Hebrews 3:14). Today you are hearing His voice and being introduced to the mysteries of God. Harden not your heart. Boldly enter the promised rest. (Hebrews 4:7)

This *strong meat* that I am sharing **"…belongeth to them that are of full age, even those who by reason of use have their senses exercised to discern both good and evil."** (Hebrews 5:14)

"That ye be not slothful, but followers of them who through faith and patience inherit the promise." (Hebrews 6:12)

Reconciliation is the act or process of restoring harmony and unity in a broken relationship. (Essential Bible Dictionary, 2011) As we noted earlier, the disobedience of Adam and Eve broke man's relationship with God. Reconciliation supposes a quarrel or breach of friendship. Sin causes the sinner to have enmity with God, and God is justly offended with the sinner.

The scriptures contain the word of reconciliation. The scriptures show us that peace was made by the blood of Jesus. 2 Corinthians 5:20 speaks of reconciliation as our duty. This is man's ultimate task.

Our ministry is the ministry of reconciliation, as we walk in the footsteps of Jesus. We must reconcile the carnal mind with the Spirit of God within us. We do so by employing the Word of God. With reconciliation as our goal – with unity and harmony set before us, we press towards the high calling. Paul writes in Philippians 3:14-15:

"I press toward the mark for the prize of the high calling of God in Christ Jesus.

Let us therefore, as many as be perfect, be thus minded: and if in any thing ye be otherwise minded, God shall reveal even this unto you."

The high calling is to full reconciliation of the mind and Spirit, with the Spirit taking the lead in all matters. Greater is he that is in us than he that is in the world. God is in us. The carnal mind is in and of the world.

Once you realize who you are and what you are through Jesus' redemptive work, you realize that you are perfectly made. You are a perfect example of the new species God intended. You are a man or woman with God living on the inside.

That is what Paul means when he says: **"…as many as be perfect"** in verse 15. If you don't see yourself as the Righteousness of God – sanctified and set apart for God's service; you find it difficult to stand in the presence of the Father without guilt and shame. Once you know your true perfection, you confidently ask your Father for assistance. And if you have difficulty with some concepts associated with your perfection, God will reveal it to you. Because you are His child, and He wants you to succeed in the reconciliation task.

Pray: **Dear Father, help us to understand and be complete in our ministry of reconciliation.**

Once the Spirit takes rulership in our lives, we will walk as Jesus walked.

"Believest thou not that I am in the Father, and the Father in me? The words that I speak unto you I speak not of myself: but the Father that dwelleth in me, he doeth the works.

Believe me that I am in the Father, and the Father in me: or else believe me for the very works' sake.

Verily, verily I say unto you, He that believeth on me, the works that I do shall he do also; and greater works than these shall he do; because I go unto my Father." (John 14: 10-12)

I believe Jesus is saying: Believe what I just told you – I am in the Father and the Father is in me. Believe I am not speaking or acting on my own – but because the Father lives in Me. Believe He speaks and He does the works through my human body.

If you will only believe this brothers and sisters, you will realize that the Father now dwells in you, as He dwells in Jesus. You can do even greater works than Jesus did.

CHAPTER 10

THE NATURE OF GOD IN MAN

To review, the redemptive work of Jesus Christ was a matter of substitution. Chapter 6 reviewed the substitutions that were made by the finished work of Jesus as well as the work still required by each man/woman's individual effort.

According to Webster's International Dictionary (1961), Nature is "the normal and characteristic quality, strength, vigor, or resiliency; the essential character or constitution of something; the essence or ultimate form of something; the distinguishing properties or qualities of something; a creative and controlling agent, force, or principle operating in something and determining wholly or chiefly its constitution, development, and well-being".

The essence or distinguishing property of God is LOVE. The controlling force or principle operating in God is LOVE. The ultimate form and essential character of God is LOVE.

I have noticed that there are few teachings in the modern church about love. Love is mentioned in a cursory manor, but rarely delved into as a really important principle of Christianity. I have never heard or witnessed a major teaching or a conference revolving around LOVE.

John 3:16 reads: **"For God so loved the world, that he gave his only begotten Son, that whosoever believeth in him should not perish, but have everlasting life."** God loved mankind so much, despite mankind's many failings – from Adam and Eve to the cross.

"God is love; and he that dwelleth in love dwelleth in God, and God in him" (1John 4:16b)

"Herein is love, not that we loved God, but that he loved us, and sent his Son to be the propitiation for our sins" (1 John 4:10)

God has always loved man, despite the many disappointments presented by the sense-oriented, dead-spirited specimens presented throughout the Bible. God has always loved man despite the confused, half-Christians that walk the earth today. What is a half-Christian? A man or women who has verbally accepted and confessed Jesus Christ as Lord and Savior, who has received the gift of Eternal Life and had the dead spirit replaced by the Nature of God – which is love.

However, this half-Christian is not living in the fullness of his/her "Jesus-within-mindedness" (Kenyon, 2011), because they have not known and/or believed in the reality of their redemption. Furthermore, they have not proceeded to renew their minds. Therefore, they reside on the borders of Christianity, not reaping the benefits of redemption – no power, no spiritual growth, no perception of their redemption, wisdom, righteousness and sanctification. God forbid!

No wonder the Church is standing ineffective in the world today. It is comprised by a majority of half-Christians whose growth and development has been stunted by inadequate spiritual teaching. The flocks are being fed nothing but pablum/milk. They are force-fed sin-consciousness, guilt, and "worthlessness in the sight of God". They have not been gradually moved to the meat of the Word. The same old lessons and examples are recycled.

The fullness of redemption, as the result of salvation, is not taught. So today's Christians feel like they are a bunch of "sinners saved by grace" -- spiritual weaklings. They fear God and they fear the devil. They fear demons and the powers of darkness – all because they do not know who they are. They may have been told that they are the Righteousness of God, but what that entails is not fully explained. Therefore it is not understood.

They are not told that they can now stand in the presence of the Father without any consciousness of inferiority – because they are the Righteousness of God. That old person, burdened with sin and guilt, is gone. They have not been informed that they are new creatures/new creations, a new species of man and woman. The words have been said, but the meaning behind the words has not been clarified. Is this because the teachers, and preachers, and prophets themselves do not know the fullness of redemption? I don't know the answer to that. But if they know and understand the matter fully, they best be teaching it fully or be in danger of hell fire!

These half-Christians are not told that God has set them aside for a specific task – to show His love in this earth, to be instruments of His love in this earth. They are too concerned about being teachers, and prophets, and evangelists, and pastors.

They are too worried about titles – when their main assignment is to LOVE. Jesus told the disciples what the two commandments are under the New Covenant.

Much simpler than the heavy burdens of the Mosaic Law and the intricate ordinances of the Old Testament – Jesus condensed our tasks to two simple commandments.

One of the scribes asked Jesus, **"Which is the first commandment of all?"**

Jesus answered in Mark 12:29-31: **"…The first of all the commandments is, Hear, O Israel; The Lord our God is one Lord:**

And thou shalt love the Lord thy God with all thy heart, and with all thy soul, and with all thy mind, and with all thy strength: this is the first commandment.

And the second is like, namely this, Thou shalt love thy neighbour as thyself. There is none other commandment greater than these."

Loving my neighbor as much as I love myself is a tall order. Yes it is, if you're doing it based on your own strength and the carnal mind. **"And hope maketh not ashamed; because the love of God is shed abroad in our hearts by the Holy Ghost which is given unto us."** (Romans 5:5) Part of our redemption package is the removal of a dead spirit caused by separation from God – and the insertion of the Nature of God, which is LOVE. Now the ability of God is at work within us. **"Now unto him that is able to do exceeding abundantly above all that we ask or think, according to the power that worketh in us"** (Ephesians 3:20). The power of God's love is working in us and through us now. Immediately following, Ephesians 4:1-2 says: **"I therefore the prisoner of the Lord, beseech you that ye walk worthy of the vocation wherewith ye are called,**

With all lowliness and meekness, with longsuffering, forbearing one another in love;…"

Per Paul, we are called to this vocation. A vocation is "a summons or strong inclination to a particular state or course of action; a divine call to the religious life; occupation…" (Webster , 2006) Our occupation and divine calling is to LOVE. That love flows from the love "shed abroad in our hearts" by the Holy Ghost, or the Spirit of God.

The carnal mind will stand to block this heretofore forbidden act of LOVE. The dead spirit of the Old Covenant could not attain this feat of loving so indiscriminately. However, the new creation, the new species men and women are equipped with the Love of God, God's Nature, placed inside their spirit place. As the mind is renewed, it will submit more and more to the Spirit of God within -- being re-shaped, remodeled, and elevated to spiritual awareness and reverence.

This renewal is accomplished by reading/hearing, studying, meditating and living the Word of God. It's a process – not accomplished overnight, but yet accomplishable with earnest desire and dependence on the Holy Spirit. The Christian must realize that all the scriptures surrounding his/her redemption are true and applicable NOW.

"Ye are of God, my little children, and have overcome them: because greater is he that is in you than he that is in the world." (1 John 4:4)

"No man hath seen God at any time. If we love one another, God dwelleth in us, and his love is perfected in us." (1 John 4:12) The world can see God through our love one for another. In John 13:34-35 Jesus states; **"A new commandment I give unto you, That ye love one another; as I have loved you, that ye also love one another.**

By this shall all men know that ye are my disciples, if ye have love one to another."

Each Christian who is born again must realize that he/she is the Righteousness of God and that God's love nature abides in him/her. But in order to activate this love nature and the power associated with it, the Christian must begin the work of renewing his/her mind. The gifts of redemption are free, but man must tame and subdue that carnal, sense-driven, mind with washing of water by the word.- Ephesians 5:25-27 says: **"…even as Christ also loved the church, and gave himself for it,**

That he might sanctify and cleanse it with the washing of water by the word,

That he might present it to himself a glorious church, not having spot, or wrinkle, or any such thing; but that it should be holy and without blemish."

The Word of God will do the work, but it is up to each Christian to daily expose the mind to the Word of God through reading/hearing, studying, meditating, and living the Word. Each individual Christian must tame his own id and ego with the guidance of the Word of God. The man or woman of God is Spirit-led. The man or woman of God walks by faith and not by sight. (2 Corinthians 5:7)

The love I speak of here is not the wishy-washy, kissy-huggy, loyal-to-the-end, ride-or-die definitions of today's world. We are not discussing here romantic love or deep friendship. Agape is unconditional love. **Agape Love is treating the other human being as you want to be treated.** Love is not giving all you own away and making yourself homeless and poverty-stricken. But love is sharing what you do have with others. That may be money or possessions. That may be a helping hand. That may be kind words. That may be respect. That may be a "thank you". That may be acknowledgement of another's presence. That may be acknowledgement of another's contribution. Love is wanting to help your fellow man find the salvation you have found.

Love is having no respect of persons – treating the rich man one way and the poor man differently; treating the powerful man one way, and the powerless person differently. James 2:9 says: **"But if ye have respect to persons, ye commit sin, and are convinced of the law as transgressors."** Here James is referring to what he called the royal law in James 2:8 – **"Thou shalt love thy neighbour as thyself,…"**. Jesus was not impressed by titles, education levels, or riches – but He loved them all. So much so, that He died for them all.

CHAPTER 11

CHRIST IN YOU — THE MYSTERY REVEALED

There is a mystery that was hidden for ages and generations. This mystery was opened up to Paul, and Paul shares the mystery with believers in his epistles. I believe the mystery was revealed to Paul because he was a Bible scholar in his time. He knew the Word of God (the portion revealed to man in that time) inside and out. He had studied for years under the tutorship of Gamaliel. Because of his indepth familiarity with God's Word, and Paul's sincere desire to serve God, Paul was chosen to see and understand the mystery.

To become privy to the understanding of the mystery, the born-again Christian must:

"…continue in the faith grounded and settled, and be not moved away from the hope of the gospel, which ye have heard, and which was preached to every creature which is under the heaven, whereof I Paul am made a minister." (Colossians 1:23)

In Colossians 1:26-27 Paul unfolds the mystery:

"Even the mystery which hath been hid from ages and from generations, but now is made manifest to his saints:

To whom God would make known what is the riches of the glory of this mystery among the Gentiles; which is Christ in you, the hope of glory."

Per the *Life Point* in Joyce Meyers' Amplified Bible, page 1967): *"Glory is the manifestation of God's excellence and goodness. We all want glory, but we can only hope to experience it because of God's presence in our lives as believers in Jesus Christ. That is what Paul talks about in Colossians 1:27.*

Christ must live in us; otherwise there is no hope of our ever experiencing the glory of God. We can look forward to new realms of glory on a continual basis because of His grace and favor, which He gives to those who believe. Rejoice in the Hope of glory, which is Christ in you.

Per a note on page 1966 of Joyce Meyers' Amplified Bible (1987):

Colossians 1:26-27 tells us that Christ 'within and among' us is the Hope of glory. You and I can only realize and experience the glory of God in our lives because Christ is in us. He is our hope of seeing better things.

The glory of God is His manifested excellence. As the children of God, we have a blood-bought right to experience the best God has planned for us. Satan furiously fights the plan of God in each of our lives, and his primary weapon is deception.

When we are deceived, we believe something that is not true. Even though it is not true, it seems true to us because that is what we believe.

Much of the time we feel defeated as we look at ourselves and our lack of ability. What we need to do is remember that Christ in us is our 'Hope [of realizing] the glory.' – **the manifested excellence of God**.

Man longs to see the glory of God. Christians, especially yearn to see and experience the glory of God. What is His glory? His glory is experiencing the manifestation of God's excellence (His superiority, perfection, virtue, merit, power). Watching the blind man regain his sight; watching the lame boy walk; watching demons flee from a possessed person; watching five thousand being fed with five fish and two loaves; watching the walls of Jericho fall by the sound of praise and worship; watching the Red Sea open and become dry land for the people of God to cross – these are manifestations of the excellence (glory) of God. They can still be experienced in this day and this time, if only the born-again Christians would realize the reality of redemption.

You are the Righteousness of God. You are sanctified and set apart. You have access to God's wisdom. You are fully redeemed from sin, guilt, and condemnation. A seed of Jesus lives within you. (God knows you could not withstand a sudden influx of the fully-developed presence of Jesus' being and power – neither physically nor psychologically.) You can nurture the growth and strength of that inner being by feeding heartily on the Word of God – a gradual and progressive maturation. Just like a pregnant woman eating for the health and well-being of her unborn child, you feed on God's Word. Then the miracle can happen. You become a mighty vessel of God – as the Spirit of God (Jesus) within you grows and takes command of your life, of your words and actions. All must be filtered through and directed by the Spirit of God within you.

Then you can speak to the storm – and it must cease. Then you can usher light into every situation of which you are a part. Then you will become the salt of the earth. Then you can speak healing and deliverance and peace wherever you walk. Then you are a vessel of Love in the earth. You are not great, but greater is He that is in you than he that is in the world. He is greater than any war, any famine, any plague. You are the container for that power. Know that when you speak, it is not you speaking. You cannot claim one iota of credit for the result, because it is Jesus speaking through you. No room for personal pride – you are merely a vessel of Jesus Christ. You are no longer a mere man or mere woman. Satan's whispers of accusation no longer affect you. You **KNOW** he is a liar – for you are the Righteousness of God in Jesus Christ. You abide in Jesus and Jesus lives in you.

You are the product of the finished work of Jesus Christ. To the Lamb of God goes the victory! Amen and amen.

Imagine the power available when hundreds and thousands of born-again Christians unite in the common purpose of spreading the gospel of Jesus Christ and manifesting the Sons of God in the earth! Manifesting the Love of God into the earth realm!

"For the earnest expectation of the creature waiteth for the manifestation of the sons of God." (Romans 8:19 KJV)

"For [even the whole] creation (all nature) waits expectantly and longs earnestly for God's sons to be made known [waits for the revealing, the disclosing of their sonship]. (Romans 8:19 AMP)

CHAPTER 12

MERE MEN AND WOMEN...

Do you love Jesus? Do you love Him in word and deed? Do you love Him in spirit and in truth? Remember He said: **"If a man loves me, he will keep my word, and the Father and I will love him, and we will come and make our abode with him."** (John 14:23)

This means that God will come and live with you and in you. This means He is in your body. Wherever you go, He is with you and in you. If you are born again, this is a fact, a reality – but it must be realized and believed by you to be effective. If you don't know or don't believe it, you are a mere man or mere woman. You have the potential for a powerful existence in this world -- but because you don't know your content, your potential -- you walk the earth as a mere man or woman; just like your unsaved brethren who are lost in darkness. The light is in you, but you don't let it shine, because you don't know or you don't believe it is there.

Pray right now: **Father, help me to know, to understand, and to acknowledge Your presence within me. I welcome you into my heart and into the deeper recesses of my being. I believe. In Your Word you**

tell me: "Fear thou not, for I am with thee; be not dismayed, for I am thy God; I will strengthen thee:yea, I will help thee; yea, I will uphold thee with the right hand of my righteousness." (Isaiah 41:10)

Jesus within us brings our hope of realizing the glory -- God's manifested excellence. The same Spirit that raised Jesus from the dead dwells in you. (Romans 8:11) This Spirit heals you, makes you stronger, and gives you the consciousness of a victor and an overcomer.

No matter what the circumstances; no matter what the trial; -- confess and believe that Christ and the nature of the Father are inside of you. Where you walk, God walks with you. You have His nature of love and mercy. You have healing and deliverance power within you – not that **you** will heal or deliver; but you carry the power to the problem by His presence in you. You are the vehicle that moves God's power to the various situations in this world. Your prayers and your faith bring the atmosphere of God's presence wherever you go. That Holy atmosphere breaks every chain welded by the powers of darkness. Speak the Word of God to the challenges. Your faith and the Word will do the work.

God will work **through** you. You become the tool of His divine will on earth.

You are the spiritual ambassador who delivers God's goodness – His manifest excellence – His healing, His deliverance, His miraculous works – to those in need.

Peter was a wimp before he received the Holy Spirit within, at Pentecost. He was such a wimp that he denied knowing Christ three times before the cock crowed the next morning.

Once Peter received the gift of the Holy Ghost (Holy Spirit) on the Day of Pentecost – he became a bold witness and bearer of "Jesus-within-me". (Acts 2:14-16) In verse 16 Peter shares: **"And his name through faith in his name hath made this man strong, whom ye see and know: yea, the faith which is by him hath given him this perfect soundness in the presence of you all."** Peter was admitting: "I was a wimp a few days ago. You all know me. I'm one of you. But now his name and my faith (which come from God) have given me perfect soundness. I'm not afraid of you all. God's nature is in me and I speak boldly."

Peter knew he had received the Holy Spirit because it was evidenced by speaking in a tongue that was unknown to him. This experience gave Peter the confirmation of an inner change and the courage necessary to work so boldly for God. I believe receipt of the Holy Spirit is not dependent on speaking in tongues; but that the evidence of speaking in tongues really reinforces to the carnal mind that God now abides within, in the form of the Holy Spirit. Speaking in tongues is an outward confirmation of an inner change.

I believe the Spirit enters all born-again Christians – whether silently or with the evidence of speaking in tongues. Confirmation is a bonus that allows the Christian to speak and act boldly. Confirmation, I believe, engenders a greater measure of faith in the born-again Christian.

Jesus promised the gift of the Holy Spirit. Once the Christian speaks in tongues, he/she knows, without any doubt, that the Holy Spirit dwells within. Without that evidence, the enemy can constantly chatter and cast doubt that the Christian's salvation is complete – thereby creating an avenue for doubt in the mind and heart of the Christian.

Speaking in tongues is a gift available to the born-again Christian by merely asking for it. Why not ask today? If you believe, you will receive. If it takes awhile, keep the faith. Read the Word about the Holy Ghost. You can also ask a tongue- speaking brother or sister to assist you. It's a free gift, available to every born-again Christian. I believe you can serve God without it, but it's much easier with indisputable confirmation.

Furthermore, the gift of tongues provides a new prayer language that satan cannot understand – nor can he circumvent. When you don't know what to pray in your native language, you can allow the Holy Spirit to pray for the situation in your prayer language. This baffles satan, because he won't know how to attack your requests.

"Likewise the Spirit also helpeth our infirmities: for we know not what we should pray for as we ought: but the Spirit itself maketh intercession for us with groanings which cannot be uttered.

And he that searcheth the hearts knoweth what is the mind of the Spirit, because he maketh intercession for the saints according to the will of God."(Romans 8: 26-27)

CHAPTER 13

RENEWAL OF THE MIND: THE HARD WAY VS EASIERWAY

Romans 12:2 is the basis for this chapter. Although renewal of the mind has been mentioned previously in this book, I will now elaborate on the topic.

"And be not conformed to this world: but be ye transformed by the renewing of your mind, that ye may prove what is that good, and acceptable, and perfect, will of God."

"Renewing of your mind" is one of those Christian jargon terms that is often spoken, but seldom explained. Without knowing its meaning and importance, the term is thrown about in sermon after sermon, and teaching after teaching – until it has become trite; a once effective phrase/idea spoiled from long familiarity and overuse. (Websters 2006)

Christianity has received a bad reputation, because so many of those who profess to be Christians are not acting like Christians. Unfortunately many seem hypocritical, as they profess one set of morals, but they live another. The lifestyles of many Christians cannot be distinguished from that of their "unsaved" counterparts. These "half-Christians" are still lying, cheating, stealing, fornicating, using illegal drugs, committing adultery, etc. Yet they go to church every Sunday and Bible Class every Wednesday. These "half-Christians" sing in the choir and serve as ushers, teachers, deacons, and missionaries. Yet their lives are not clean, and they are not approaching holiness. Why?

Whenever you see a man or woman who proclaims to be a Christian – but that person is mean-spirited, dishonest, or living a morally-questionable lifestyle; don't discount Christianity as a whole. **That person** has a problem. What problem Sister Jannah? That person has not renewed his/her mind. That person is living in a spiritual rut, somewhere between half-Christian and full Christian. If born again, that person has God on the inside and has been given eternal life – but the flesh- driven carnal mind is still in charge of their behaviors. Since this is rarely taught and explained to the new Christian, this half-Christian may think that he/she is perfectly fine – despite the internal conflict they experience as sin-consciousness. They can't figure out why they are unable to change those old habits and those old thought patterns. This is the dilemma of half-Christians: **"For that which I do I allow not: for what I would, that do I not; but what I hate, that do I."** (Romans 7:15)

Remember Paul saying: **"For I know that in me (that is, in my flesh,) dwelleth no good thing: for to will is present with me; but how to perform that which is good I find not.**

For the good that I would I do not: but the evil which I would not, that I do. I find then a law, that, when I would do good, evil is present with me.

For I delight in the law of God after the inward man:

But I see another law in my members, warring against the law of my mind, and bringing me into captivity to the law of sin which is in my members.“ (Romans 7:18-19, 21-23)

The sin is in the flesh – the old habits and thought patterns of the carnal mind. The flesh is composed of our five senses. We have followed the commands and “wisdom” of the flesh since we were born. We have always “believed” the flesh. We have always believed the interpretations of our five senses, linked with our fleshly experiences.

Once born again, the Christian is a new creature, a new creation. However, that carnal mind is still in control of the body. The new Christian has a new Spirit within; but the flesh-driven carnal mind is still wielding the power of control of the physical body. The goal is for the Spirit to take control of the physical body and the thought processes. This can only happen as the mind of the Christian is renewed. The renewed mind takes on power and strength. The renewed mind eventually takes full control of the Christian’s thoughts and actions. The Christian walks by faith, and not by sight (the senses). Decisions are made along spiritual lines, instead of carnal guidance. Actions are directed by the Spirit within, not by mere reaction to old habits.

So the half-Christian is warring on his/her own against all the old habits and thought patterns imported from the old creature. This is a battle that a mere human cannot win. The half-Christian needs help, serious help that can only be accomplished with renewal of that old carnal mind and development of the inner man.

"That he would grant you, according to the riches of his glory, to be strengthened with might by his Spirit in the inner man;

That Christ may dwell in your hearts by faith; that ye being rooted and grounded in love,

May be able to comprehend with all saints what is the breadth, and length, and depth, and height;

And to know the love of Christ, which, passeth knowledge, that ye might befilled with all the fulness of God." (Ephesians 3:16-19)

Renewal of the mind is not an **option**. Renewal of the mind is a **requirement** for the Christian to have power over him- or herself, and over circumstances.

Otherwise the battle will continue with the half-Christian doing what he/she hates instead of what he/she really wants to do.

The goal of the Christian is the fullness of God through spiritual vs carnal control. That is the only way to full Christianhood which allows us to **"walk worthy of the vocation wherewith we are called"** (Ephesians 4:1)

How do I renew my mind? That is a common question. The answer seems too simple to be true. Man tends to make all spiritual things really hard to attain. But God has made it simple. All a man or woman has to do is this: hear/read the Word of God, study and meditate on that Word, and then live the Word. Then what?

Then nothing. Just do that!

It can't be that simple! It is that simple. But you have to believe in the power of God's Word. The Word will do the work. You don't have to fight. Let the Word in your mind, your heart, and your mouth wage the battle. The desire for old habits and relationships will dissipate. Unholy and unwholesome thought patterns will fade away. Addictions will become distasteful. When they raise their ugly heads, you just speak the Word to them – just as Jesus did in the wilderness. (Luke 4)

You may experience impatience or discontent as you begin your trek through God's Word. Some portions may seem boring and irrelevant to your purpose.

Here you **can** use your willpower – to keep your body in the reading posture long enough to consume that chapter. At first, it might all sound like jibberish. That's how it sounded to me in 2000 when I returned to the faith. But I just continued to read and study. Also listening to various sermons and teachings can help – as they often explain some of the passages you encounter. Bible study groups or a prayer partner can help in opening up meanings for you. What's important is that you stick with it. Don't give up! The devil wants you to give up. He knows the end results of your faithful endeavor, and he doesn't want you to reach it. Of course, there is really no end, but it becomes easier as you go.

The Word is so good that you will grow to love it. You will reap a new meaning to a familiar verse every time that you reread it. The Word never grows old or stale. It is always fresh. The Word is alive and life-giving. The deeper and longer that you pursue the Word and understanding, the more powerful your inner man becomes. Gradually that inner man will begin to take command in your life. That inner man is Jesus-within-you – God's nature of love inside of you. Christ in you – the hope of glory!

CHAPTER 14

WHAT MUST I DO TO BE SAVED? ACCEPT YOUR INHERITANCE

Joining a church, accepting Jesus Christ as Lord and Savior, being water-baptized and receiving the Holy Spirit – this is just the beginning of your journey as a new creation.

Next comes your hearing, reading,, studying, meditating, and living God's Word – on a daily basis. You must regularly feed on God's Word. God's Word provides all you need for spiritual growth and development. As your inner man becomes stronger, the Spirit within will automatically move into a position of leadership in your life.

The transitions may seem seamless to your conscious mind, but there will be days when you wake up and say, "I'm different than I was last week. I handle stressful situations more calmly than I used to. I find myself leaning on the Everlasting Arms more often than on my own problem-solving skills. I don't feel the need to win arguments, for only God's Word is true. I don't worry about my health, because the healer is inside me and will quicken this mortal body. I don't mind that people talk about me and think I'm strange. I'm a child of the King. I am royalty. I don't have to worry about rent and bills because my God provides all my need according to His riches in glory. The Lord is my Shepherd and I shall not want."

Your new assignment is the Word of God. It is through study, meditation and living of the Word that you will attain your spiritual goals. You have fulfilled the physical goals of confessing Jesus Christ as Lord and Savior, baptism, and receipt of the Holy Spirit. From here on, your goals are spiritual. This is the way that you will be able to let God's power work through you. This is how you will be able to keep the commandments of Love – passionately loving God and your neighbor as yourself.

Through the ages, men have made it sound hard to realize the God in you. Men have advocated for all kinds of rituals – even painful ones, to assure your salvation.

God is a fair God and a loving God. He simply asks that you hear, read, study, meditate, and live His Word. The Word by its power will renew your mind. The Spirit within you, God's Spirit, will take over your life as the power of God works **in** you and **through** you to others.

By ministering to others the ministry of reconciliation, the Church will become the most powerful organization on this planet – and the only entity that can save this planet. For with God, all things are possible.

You are needed as an individual and as a part of the collective Body of Christ. Never underestimate the power of a born-again, fully woke Christian.

Jesus spoke in John 10:10: **"I am come that they might have life, and that they might have it more abundantly."** The Greek word for Life is *Zoe*. *Zoe* means "God's nature, God's substance, God's being…" (Kenyon, 2011) Jesus' intention was to help establish God's nature and substance within every man or woman who will believe on Him – on Jesus' life, death, and resurrection – on Jesus' established seat at the right hand of the Father. Per Kenyon (2011, p. 79): *The Father's dream is to reproduce Himself in us.*

Physical body knowledge is all a man has prior to being born again. All of his knowledge comes through the five senses (the flesh). Sense-knowledge can never find God, nor understand spiritual things.

"For they that are after the flesh [senses, carnal] do mind the things of the flesh [senses, carnal], but they that are after the Spirit the things of the Spirit.

For to be carnally minded is death; but to be spiritually minded is life and peace.

Because the carnal mind is enmity against God: for it is not subject to the law [Word] of God, neither can be.

So then they that are in the flesh [carnal minded, sense-ruled] cannot please God." (Romans 8:5-8)

When the Christian is born again, he/she automatically receives Eternal Life, Zoe and the Nature of God within. The Christian becomes a partaker of the Divine Nature. What is the Divine Nature? It is Love. According to Kenyon (2011, p.104), this Jesus Nature makes you a dominant personality, a Master personality.

Jesus Nature? I thought you said Divine Nature or the Nature of God. Do not lose sight that the Father and the Son are one.

Jesus was a human man with God living on the inside of Him. He lived a perfect life. Jesus came to earth and died on the cross that all of our sins might be remitted, or wiped out, as if they never existed. Therefore, when a man or woman accepts Jesus Christ as Lord and Savior – all sins are remitted. That person can legally receive the Nature of God. That person, like Jesus, is now a new creation – a human man or woman with God living on the inside of him or her. This new Christian is a replica of Jesus. Through this redemptive process, Jesus obeyed the primal commandment of God – be fruitful and multiply. The New Christian needs only to renew his/her mind so that he/she can take on the MIND OF CHRIST. (1 Corinthians 2:16) **Then! – Watch out satan! All power in heaven and in earth lies in the members of the Body of Christ knowing and accepting the reality of redemption.**

You, my born-again Christian friend, are a joint heir with Christ. You have inherited all that an heir receives. Because you are born of the Spirit, you are now spirit. You no longer belong to the Old Order – you belong to the Family of God. You are in the realm of Life (Zoe), Eternal Life; not death. Also you now have the ability to enjoy your inheritance. **"Giving thanks unto the Father, which hath made us meet to be partakers of the**

inheritance of the saints in light: Who hath delivered us from the power of darkness and hath translated us into the kingdom of his dear son: In whom we have redemption through his blood, even the forgiveness of sins:" (Colossians 1:12-14)

"And of his fulness have all we received, and grace for grace." (John 1:16)

This new status of grace means absolutely nothing if you don't take advantage of it. The fullness is probably undeveloped or under-developed in You. You have a choice – whether you will or will not grab hold of "the riches of his glory". Per Romans 9:23**: "And that he might make known the riches of his glory on the vessels of mercy, which he had afore prepared unto glory."** Jesus wants to make known His manifest excellence through us, His vessels of mercy (created by His mercy) who He has prepared for manifestation of His glory. Hallelujah!

Praise Almighty God!

If you are not taking advantage of your inheritance, you are a half-Christian; always struggling to get something or be something. Please realize that you were created in Christ: **"For we are his workmanship, created in Christ Jesus for good works, which God afore prepared that we should walk in them."** (Ephesians 2:10)

Once born again, the sin problem is settled for the believer. The new problem is the Christian entering into his/her inheritance.

CHAPTER 15

WHY THE MYSTERY

Satan was fooled into plotting the crucifixion of Jesus Christ. Had he known what he was actually doing, he would have refrained. The scriptures make it very clear.

Paul said of the mystery: **"But we speak the wisdom of God, in a mystery, even the hidden wisdom, which God ordained before the world unto our glory.**

Which none of the princes of this world knew: for had they known it, they would not have crucified the Lord of glory." (1 Corinthians 2:7-8)

Had satan known the outcome of his "plot", he would not have supported the death of Jesus Christ. For Jesus' life, death, and resurrection established the clemency of mankind. Jesus' finished work satisfied all of the universally-established, God- ordained, legal requirements for the eradication of mankind's sins and trespasses. This finished work nailed all of the impossible-to-obey ordinances to the cross and birthed mankind into a new period of sinlessness – pure as the driven snow.

"Blotting out the handwriting of ordinances that was against us, which was contrary to us, and took it out of the way, nailing it to his cross." (Colossians 2:14)

Oh Happy Day! All a man or woman has to do is accept Jesus Christ as Lord and Savior. Repentance is included in that act. It signals that "Lord I have tried living without you, but now I know that I need you. In order to become who I really am, a spiritual being, I need your guidance."

Satan is the god of this world. He has blinded the minds of the unbelievers with sense (carnal) wisdom, philosophy, theosophy, devil worship, necromancy, voodoo – and a million other distortions. **"In whom the god of this world hath blinded the minds of them which believe not, lest the light of the glorious gospel of Christ, who is the image of God, should shine unto them."** (2 Corinthians 4:4)

Furthermore, satan has blinded the eyes of born-again Christians by deception and a show of false power. He has manipulated Christians into believing that they are worthless, hopeless, powerless beings. He has deceived Christians into believing that they should fear him (satan) – when Jesus defeated satan and the kingdom of darkness during his three-day hiatus after the cross.

"And having spoiled principalities and powers, he (Jesus) made a show of them openly, triumphing over them in it." (Colossians 2:15)

Christians are so fooled that they don't even know that Jesus is right there inside of them – ready to perform all of the miraculous works he performed, and more.

Born-again Christians, whose sins have been remitted fully, are still feeling guilt and shame from old trespasses.

Wake up Brothers and Sisters! You no longer have to wallow in a pit of imagined weakness and lack of power. All of the power you need is inside of you. To unlock it: read, hear, study, meditate, and live the Word of God. Sounds too simple?! That's how the devil deceives you. He wants it to sound complicated.

He wants you to go sit atop a mountain somewhere and contemplate your ignorance. He does not want you out in the world – active and powerful, speaking healing, deliverance, freedom to all. He wants you to follow a guru or join a cult, or try to buy your way into Eternal Life through prosperity teachings. You already have Eternal Life with your acceptance of Jesus Christ as Lord and Savior. You are the Righteousness of God. You are a member of the Family of God. You are a son of God. God can work in you and through you, if you will allow Him to do so.

But you must know who you are. You must realize the reality of your redemption. It is more than a few acts of faith – confession, baptism, receipt of the Holy Spirit. The reality of redemption requires renewal of your mind, so that you can live on the Spirit's wavelength – not that of your carnal, sense-ruled mind. The mind can be a wonderful tool, but only as an apprentice and servant of the Spirit.

God's Word is powerful. The Word is God. Believe and receive the fullness of your salvation. To do so will bless you. To do so will bless the Body of Christ. To do so will bless the world. Believe and receive the fullness of God. Christ in each of you is our hope of glory. Christ in each of you is our hope of experiencing the manifest excellence of God. Christ in each of you brings the manifestation of the Sons of God. Acknowledge the Christ in you… In Jesus' Name. Amen.

CHAPTER 16

THE BATTLE IS THE LORD'S: REMEMBER THAT

The battle is not yours, it's the Lord's. How often have we heard this in today's church. Yet each Christian tends to strive toward perfection – failing with each attempt, and thereby accentuating that ever-present sin-consciousness. 2 Chronicles 20:15 reminds us, **"… for the battle is not yours, but God's."**

YOU can't make yourself good. YOU cannot stop all of your bad habits. YOU cannot single-handedly correct all of your shortcomings. In fact, YOU don't even know what all of your failings are. If you continue to try to live under the Law of Sin and Death, you just collect a list of "don'ts" and "do's" that you will not live up to in your own strength. The Law of Sin and Death, the law as presented by Moses, could only **define and reveal sin.** The law could not **conquer and subdue sin.** (Zondervan's Matthew Henry Commentary, 1992, p. 579) So if a man is living under the banner of the Law of Sin and Death – carrying the ever-present flag of sin-consciousness; that man cannot overcome his sinful nature.

You say you believe in God. You say you believe in His Word. You say you have unwavering faith – yet you still try to change yourself, instead of putting it all into the hands of the creator.

Paul went through the same thing. You're not alone. He said when he tries to do good, his body does the opposite. Romans 7:14-25 reads:

"For we know that the law is spiritual: but I am carnal, sold under sin.

For that which I do I allow not: for what I would that do I not; but what I hate, that do I.

If then I do that which I would not, I consent unto the law that it is good. Now then it is no more I that do it, but sin that dwelleth in me.

For I know that in me (that is, in my flesh,) dwelleth no good thing: for to will is present with me; but how to perform that which is good I find not.

For the good that I would I do not: but the evil which I would not, that I do.

Now if I do that I would not, it is no more I that do it, but sin that dwelleth in me.

I find then a law, that, when I would do good, evil is present with me. For I delight in the law of God after the inward man:

But I see another law in my members, warring against the law of my mind, and bringing me into captivity to the law of sin which is in my members.

O wretched man that I am! Who shall deliver me from the body of this death?"

Paul is basically saying that he did not have the power, on his own, to make his body do what he wanted it to do. Evil was ever-present, even though Paul delighted in the law of God (Word of God). Paul laments these circumstances and cries, **"Who shall deliver me from the body of this death?"**

Paul answers the question in the next verse, verse 25: **"I thank God through Jesus Christ our Lord."** God shall deliver me from the cruel reign of the body and the carnal mind – through Jesus Christ our Lord. It is only through the finished work of Jesus that man has a portal of entry into a sinless life – void of rule by the flesh and fleshly desires and carnal promptings.

None of us humans has the power on our own to defeat the wiles of the devil, the cravings of the flesh, long-practiced evil habits, second-nature reactions to certain stimuli, persuasive perversions, temptations to evil behavior, pagan rituals long-practiced, soul ties, and generational curses. Jesus Christ has already overcome the world. Jesus Christ, living in the born-again Christian, has already defeated and will continue to defeat the enemy on our behalf.

Jesus lived on this earth, in a human body. So he understands the temptations and agony of confronting human foibles, failures and emotions on a minute-by-minute basis. Jesus understands. **"For we have not an high priest which cannot be touched with the feeling of our infirmities; but was in all points tempted like as we are, yet without sin."** (Hebrew 4:15)

Infirmity, according to Webster's Dictionary (2006) means: *"…condition of being feeble: frailty, disease, malady; personal failing; weak of mind, will, or character; irresolute; vacillating."* How well this definition describes many new -- and old Christians.

But you are not left to fight the good fight alone. Jesus understands. He experienced living in a human body. As a born-again Christian, as a new creature in Christ, you have Jesus living inside of you. Lean and depend on Jesus to remove unhealthy and sinful habits and tendencies. Lean on Jesus to get rid of all that fleshly, carnal garbage in your life. You cannot do it alone.

Only through Jesus Christ can you be a conqueror of the otherwise unconquerable.

How can you believe in a Saviour who can single-handedly, in one fell swoop, erase your past sins and trespasses? How can you say you believe in a God who has that kind of power – and at the same time think that He would leave you helpless in your battle against sin? He would not. He did not. Your moment of salvation was the first big step towards liberty from sin, but it is not the final rung on your ladder to heaven.

The one offensive weapon given to each Christian is the sword of the Spirit, the Word of God. This weapon is not fully utilized. Many Christians feel it is only to fight off the wiles and attacks of the enemy. This is not so. The Word is our "spiritual Wheaties" – the breakfast, lunch, and dinner of God's champions. The Christian must ingest, ruminate, digest, and meditate God's Word daily. God's Word is Spirit and Life. God's Word gives the strength to overcome temptation. Jesus did not die on the cross, and then say that we need to keep ourselves until His return. He gave us the Holy Spirit and His Word.

After all Jesus tells us in John 16:33, **"…but be of good cheer; I have overcome the world."** Then in 1 John 4:4, **"…because greater is he that is in you, than he that is in the world."** Then in 1 John 5:4, **"For whatsoever is born of God overcometh the world: and this is the victory that overcometh the world, even our faith."** If you are born again, you are born of God.

You see, the same faith that you had for salvation and acceptance of Jesus Christ as your Lord and Savior – that same faith is required to overcome the evil influences and tendencies to sin that reside in your flesh and in your carnal mind. You only have to be strong in faith, knowing that the work God has started in you – He will complete.

However, you do have a part to play. First, you must have the faith, as noted above. **"Being confident of this very thing, that he which hath begun a good work in you will perform it until the day of Jesus Christ."** (Philippians 1:6) Secondly, you must fuel your quest with the Word of God. This accomplishes a double reward – washing of water by the Word, and renewal of your mind. You must believe that God can clean up your life and you must read, study, and meditate His Word. There is power in His Words.

His Words do not return to him void. **"So shall my word be that goeth forth out of my mouth: it shall not**

return unto me void, but it shall accomplish that which I please, and it shall prosper in the thing whereto I sent it." (Isaiah 55:11) Read His Word on a daily basis – even if only a few verses.

Read out loud. Let those words sink into your very spirit – into your mind and heart. Meditate silently upon what you have read today. If your reading contained instructions on how to live, ask God to help you follow those instructions. You cannot do it alone.

Many of you believe all kinds of miraculous things that are written in the Bible. You believe, at least superficially, that God can heal the sick and raise the dead. Yet, you find it hard to believe that God's Word has the power within itself to transform people and situations. Read the gospels. Jesus operated by speaking the Word. He still operates through His Word. In the beginning was the Word and the Word was with God and the Word was God. God is His Word. Read His Word. Speak His Word. Pray His Word. Live His Word, with His assistance. You can transform your life. You cannot do it on your own. Just like you could not save yourself from the shackles of sin.

In Ezekiel 12:25 God tells us about the power of His Word. **"For I am the Lord: I will speak, and the word that I shall speak shall come to pass; it shall be no more prolonged; for in your days, O rebellious house, will I say the word and will perform it, saith the Lord God."**

God will clean up your rebellious house (your sinful nature), just as He did for Paul and others in the New Testament. God will clean up your mind, your will and your emotions – from bottom to top. Just believe and have faith in God – God is His Word. Your choice is not whether or not to sin – your choice is whether or not to cast every burden (even the sin that doth so easily beset thee) on Jesus. Your choice is whether or not to have full, unflinching faith in God to clean up every aspect of your life. Do not limit God's power by your limited perception. **"…let God be true, but every man a liar".** (Romans 3:4)

Paul sums it up in two places: first Romans 6:14-15: **"For sin shall not have dominion over you: for ye are not under the law, but under grace. What then? shall we sin, because we are not under the law, but under grace?**

God forbid." Many look at grace as a license to sin. It is not. It is a license to be liberated from the sin-consciousness engendered under the Law. We should be grace-conscious which is the same as "Jesus-within-me"-consciousness. Know consciously and consistently that you walk under grace and that Jesus Christ is inside you.

Second, Paul tells us in Titus 2:14-15: **"Who gave himself for us, that he might redeem us from all iniquity, and purify unto himself a peculiar people, zealous of good works. These things speak, and exhort, and rebuke with all authority. Let no man despise thee."** Jesus gave Himself that we could be redeemed from ALL iniquity, and that we could be purified unto Him. God is on our side. God, by His loving grace will clean up your rebellious house. We can speak this boldly. We can exhort (encourage) our fellow Christians with this message. We can rebuke every insinuation of satan that we are not righteous. No man can despise God's truth concerning you.

CHAPTER 17

JESUS CAME TO MAKE IT EASIER, NOT HARDER

Jesus' life, death, and resurrection occurred to make our journey in life easier. Jesus did away with the Old Covenant, and replaced it with a better covenant. Jesus did away with the Law of Sin and Death – replacing it with the Law of the Spirit of Life in Christ Jesus. Jesus replaced our duly deserved punishment with Grace. Jesus gave us His Righteousness in place of our sin, guilt, and condemnation. Jesus took away our dead spirit and replaced it with the loving nature of Almighty God. Jesus eradicated our past sins, as if they never existed. Jesus offers forgiveness with the confession of today's missteps Our slates can remain forever clean.

When Paul approached God regarding a nagging weakness (a thorn in his flesh), Jesus told Paul: **"My grace is sufficient for thee: for my strength is made perfect in weakness."** (2 Corinthians 12:9) God gets the glory each time you overcome that nagging weakness.

Jesus replaced the Ten Commandments and over six hundred rules and ordinances in Leviticus with two simple commandments. "

"…Thou shalt love the Lord thy God with all thy heart, and with all thy soul, and with all thy mind.

This is the first and great commandment.

And the second is like unto it, Thou shalt love thy neighbour as thyself." (Matthew 22:27-39)

With the love of God in our hearts, God's Word in our mouths, eternal life assured, and unflinching faith in **ALL** of God's Word – we have all we need for victory.

CHAPTER 18

GRACE: THE REALITY OF REDEMPTION

I have not mentioned GRACE a lot in this book. I did not intend for GRACE to be a topic. However, I cannot escape the truth – that this book is a product of God's revelation, not my intellect. I asked God to give me the revelation necessary to make the reality of redemption plain for all readers. As I neared the ending of this book, God opened another door of understanding. Brothers and Sisters, I gladly share this with you.

Grace is a word that sums up the reality of our redemption. Grace is the essence of the gift we received through the finished work of our Lord and Savior, Jesus Christ.

Derek Prince defines GRACE in his book *By Grace Alone* (2013). He states *"Grace is the free, unmerited favor of God toward the undeserving and the ill-deserving."* You can't earn grace or work for it.

Grace is mentioned 155 times in the New Testament, but most modern Christians don't even bother to look up the meaning of the word, nor study the fullness of its meaning. They accept that it means "favor" and are satisfied to sing the song, *"Favor Ain't Fair", but it sure is marvellous".* That is why reading, studying, and meditating the Word of God is so important. These acts bring discernment, revelation, and understanding. Through these acts God provides us grace for grace. **"And of his fulness have all we received, and grace for grace. For the law was given by Moses, but grace and truth came by Jesus Christ."** (John 1:16-17)

What?! Yes, it even takes grace for one to believe and receive the gift of God's grace. Verse 17 makes it clear that grace came by Jesus Christ and that it is separate and different from the law of Moses. Each has its place. The Mosaic Law has its place under the Law of Sin and Death. Grace has its place as the essence of the Law of the Spirit of Life in Christ Jesus. We, born again Christians should be living under the latter – under grace.

Christians strive for righteousness, usually by works. They sing in the choir, usher, do missionary work, preach, teach, and prophesy. They speak in tongues, offer charity, pay tithes and offerings. Even though old habits and negative character traits often creep out into the arena of behavior, they are satisfied that their good works will rack up points in the heaven vs hell count.

What they don't understand is that their "righteousness" is as filthy rags to God. Their righteousness is based on trying to live under the Law of Sin and Death. Their righteousness is based on fear and guilt. It is impossible for them to fulfill all of the numerous laws, statutes, and ordinances outlined in the Bible. Few even know them all. There are over 600 in Leviticus alone.

Then add on the man-made rules of modern churches – and Wow! Who needed even more do's and don'ts.

Per Isaiah 64:6 : **"But we are all as an unclean thing, and all our righteousnesses are as filthy rags; and we do all fade as a leaf; and our iniquities, like the wind, have taken us away."**

As Paul reminds us in Romans 7, we try to do right but the flesh will not allow us to sustain ourselves in the struggle for right conduct. Our versions of righteousness are interspersed with sin. That type of righteousness is of the law. That type of righteousness gives place to the enemy to constantly accuse us of our shortcomings.

Jesus opened a new way under grace. Under grace, recognizing the reality of our redemption, we realize that we are already the righteousness of God. Our sins have been remitted. We are sanctified. We have access to the wisdom of God. There is no need for guilt, and shame, and condemnation (Romans 8:1). If we make a mistake today, we confess and wipe our slate clean once again.

We can go boldly before the throne of grace and ask according to His will – assured that we have what we ask for. No more grovelling! We are the sons of God – heirs to the promises of Abraham and joint heirs with Jesus Christ.

In Philippians 3:9 Paul says: **"And be found in him, not having mine own righteousness, which is of the law, but that which is through the faith of Christ, the righteousness which is of God by faith."** That is the righteousness we seek – the righteousness that comes as part of our salvation benefit package. This is the righteousness that was purchased by the blood of Jesus Christ. Like Abraham, our faith is imputed unto us (counted as) righteousness. Faith in what? Faith in God; faith in the finished work of Jesus Christ on our behalf; faith in the substitutionary work of Jesus; faith in the power of His Word to bring itself to pass; faith in the reality of redemption; faith in the truth of God's grace over our lives.

Rather than yielding yourself to the Law of Sin and Death – yield yourself to grace. Romans 6:16 says, **"Know ye not, that to whom ye yield yourselves servants to obey, his servants ye are to whom ye obey; whether of sin unto death, or of obedience unto righteousness?"** Live under grace. To do so is a privilege of your salvation.

CHAPTER 19

CONCLUSION

"**L**et us hear the conclusion of the whole matter. **Fear God, and keep his commandments: for this is the whole duty of man.**" (Ecclesiastes 12:13) This has always been a favorite scripture of mine, as it seems to sum up everything and anything that one might expound upon in the spiritual realm. "Fear God" means to reverence God – to show devotion and honor to; to regard as worthy of honor; to worship (pay homage); to adore (love); to admire profoundly and respectfully. (Webster, 2006) Once this is realized, then keeping His commandments completes man's duty to God.

Sister Jannah, what is the point of all that you have shared with us? What are the take-aways that I should hold close and ponder? You have spoken about many things, but what is the overarching point or conclusion that I, as the reader, should walk away with?

Dear Brother or Sister, I have asked God to give me inspiration and revelation to help me understand and share my understanding with you, on the reality of redemption. After approaching the reality myself, I knew that every Christian needs to know and understand what Jesus Christ did for them when He suffered and died on the cross – and then was resurrected and ascended into heaven. This is not the conclusion of some myth or fairytale. **This is the final resolution of a legal battle for the souls of mankind.** Jesus Christ won the suit by paying the blood price for our redemption and defeating all of the powers of darkness – including sin and death. Jesus did away with the Old Covenant and the Law of Sin and Death, and He established a New Covenant under the Law of the Spirit of Life in Christ Jesus.

This New Covenant brings rewards to any man or woman who will accept Jesus Christ as their Lord and Savior. From the moment of acceptance on, that person receives Redemption, Sanctification, access to God's Wisdom, and Righteousness. That person also receives a measure of FAITH and a measure of LOVE – seeds sown in the fertile soil of God's Nature. God's Nature of Love replaces the emptiness of the prior dead spirit. Additionally a bonus gift is the receipt of the indwelling Holy Spirit. That person becomes a member of God's Family and a joint heir with Jesus Christ. Jesus becomes his/her big brother.

I am pretty sure that most Christians do not really know what gifts they received as a result of the finished work of Jesus Christ. Unfortunately, too many Christians live in a rut of sin-consciousness – constantly beating themselves up for not living up to the Ten Commandments or any other cautionary infractions of various Bible characters. They don't know that they are the Righteousness of God, so they grovel before the throne in prayer, not believing that they are worthy of receiving the thing they pray for. They consider themselves instead as "sinners saved by grace". Actually they are the Righteousness of God living in the dispensation of Grace, where accepting and confessing Jesus as Lord and Savior makes you a new being, a new creation – a new species of human, a man or women with God on the inside of them. That is what Jesus was! That man or woman is no longer a mere man or woman. They are receptacles for the power of the Almighty – to carry that love, power, and grace all over this world.

These new creatures (2 Corinthians 5:17) are meant to carry the Love of God to their families, neighborhoods, cities, countries, and the world. This Love is a new Love, Agape. This Love is not the love of sexual attraction or brotherly friendship. This Love is the same Love that allowed Jesus Christ to die on the cross to save a wretched mankind – substituting our sin with His righteousness. (2 Corinthians 5:21) This Love is described in 1 Corinthians 13:4-7. This Love is not selfish or puffed up or prideful. This Love suffers long and is kind. This Love does not envy, is not easily provoked, seeketh not her own, thinketh no evil – believeth all things, hopeth all things, and edureth all things – rejoiceth not in iniquity but rejoiceth in the truth..

You might say: "This sounds like a chump, to me." But this is the kind of Love Jesus has for us. Do you think Jesus was a chump for dying on the cross, to give you the opportunity for Eternal Life? He was no chump! Jesus was the greatest example of Love, and the power of Love. That Love stretched through the ages – even unto this day.

What I want to emphasize is this: each Christian reader needs to know and believe that he/she has received these gifts. Each reader needs to KNOW that this is not the end of the journey. Each of us must water and cultivate the seeds of Love and Faith that were planted in our hearts when we received salvation. (Romans 5:5 and Romans 12:3) Why?

First, God replaced your dead spirit (the result of Adam and Eve's sin) with the Nature of God. He gave you His Holy Spirit. Unfortunately, your life of 12,20,30, or 40 years, has been ruled by your five senses and sense knowledge obtained from them. The five senses took over when Adam and Eve ate of the Tree of the Knowledge of Good and Evil. Man is really a spirit, just as his Father is Spirit. Man was made in the image of God, his Father. Man lost sight of his spirit when the senses (the flesh) took over in the Garden of Eden. Now, as man returns to God, through the substitutionary work of Jesus Christ, it is time for the Spirit to take charge of man's life again. The New Creation man and woman lives by the Spirit, not by sight (the senses).

In order for the seeds of Love and Faith to grow — in order for the Nature of God to take over in the New Creation Christian; in order for the Spirit to rule over the carnal mind, -- the inner man must feed on the Word of God. The inner man must read/hear, study, meditate, and live the Word of God. As this is done, the New Creation man or woman can evolve from sense/flesh rule to rule by the Spirit. The New Creation man/woman once again ascends to being the spiritual being that God created him/her to be.

Per John 1:1, **"In the beginning was the Word and the Word was with God,and the Word was God."** What an intriguing introduction to the Word!

Especially since "the Word was God". If I am to know God, I must know the Word.

Psalm 119 gives a full treatise on the Word, and its benefits for mankind. It takes 176 verses to expound upon the Word – and still its fullness is not explained.

Psalm 119 refers to the Word in several different terms. These terms are used throughout the Bible and should be acknowledged everywhere as referring to God's Word. The terms are as follows, each with a brief description from Strong's Concordance (with corresponding entry numbers for Hebrew translations).

Precept (6490) – appointed, i.e. a mandate (of God), commandment, statute

Commandment (4687) – a command whether human or divine; law, ordinance;precept

Testimony (5715) – a witness, specially a recorder

Statute (2706) – to engrave; laws being cut in stone or metal tablets; prescribe, appoint, decree

Law (8457) – a precept or statute, esp: The Decalogue or Pentateuch; from (3384) a primary root to flow as water, i.e. rain; to lay or throw (esp. an arrow; to shoot fig. to point out (as if aiming the finger) to teach, direct, inform, instruct, show

Judgment (4941) – a verdict, (favorable or unfavorable) pronounced judicially, esp. a sentence or formal decree; (8199) to judge; to pronounce sentence (for or against); to govern; condemn, defend, execute, plead, reason, rule

You may notice that the definitions of one word is another of the listed words. This is because they all refer to the same thing. They all have a similar meaning. They are all used as facets of the Word of God.

I feel so awkward explaining this. It's new to me too. But I'm willing to trust God's Word which says:

"Blessed are the undefiled in the way, who walk in the law [Word] of theLord." (Psalm 119:1)

"Wherewithal shall a young man cleanse his way? by taking heed thereto according to thy word." (Psalm 119:9)

"I will meditate in thy precepts [Word], and have respect unto thy ways. I will delight myself in thy statutes [Word]: I will not forget thy word." (Psalm 119:15-16)

"My soul cleaveth unto the dust: quicken thou me according to thy word." (Psalm 119:25)

"This is my comfort in my affliction: for thy word hath quickened me." (Psalm 119:50)

"Teach me good judgment and knowledge: for I have believed thy commandments [Word]. (Psalm 119:66)

"The law [Word] of thy mouth is better unto me than thousands of gold and silver." (Psalm 119:72)

"Let, I pray thee, thy merciful kindness be for my comfort, according to thy word unto thy servant. Let thy tender mercies come unto me, that I may live:for thy law [Word] is my delight." (Psalm 119:76-77)

"Let my heart be sound in thy statutes [Word]; that I be not ashamed." (Psalm 119:80)

"They had almost consumed me upon earth; but I forsook not thy precepts[Word]. (Psalm 119:87)

"Unless thy law [Word] had been my delights, I should then have perished in mine affliction." (Psalm 119:92)

"I will never forget thy precepts [Word]: for with them thou hast quickened me. I am thine, save me; for I have sought thy precepts [Word]. (Psalm 119:93-94)

"O how love I thy law [Word]! It is my meditation all the day." (Psalm119:97)

"Thou through thy commandments [Word] hast made me wiser than mine enemies: for they are ever with me." (Psalm 119:98)

"I have refrained my feet from every evil way, that I might keep thy word." (Psalm 119:101)

"My soul is continually in my hand: yet do I not forget thy law [Word]. (Psalm119:109)

"Deal with thy servant according unto thy mercy, and teach me thy statutes [Word]. I am thy servant; give me understanding that I may know thy testimonies [**Word**]. (Psalm 119:124-125)

"Therefore I esteem all thy precepts [Word] concerning all things to be right; and I hate every false way." (Psalm 119:128)

"The entrance of thy words giveth light; it giveth understanding unto the simple." (Psalm 119:130)

"Order my steps in thy word: and let not any iniquity have dominion over me. Deliver me from the oppression of man: so will I keep thy precepts [Word]. (Psalm 119:133)

Make thy face to shine upon thy servant; and teach me thy statutes." (Psalm 119:135)

"Thy word is very pure: therefore thy servant loveth it." (Psalm 119:140)

"Thy righteousness is an everlasting righteousness and thy law [Word] is the truth." (Psalm 119:142)

"I rejoice at thy word, as one that findeth great spoil." (Psalm 119:162)

"Great peace have they which love thy law [Word]: and nothing shall offend them." (Psalm 119:165)

"Let my cry come near before thee, O Lord: give me understanding according to thy word." (Psalm 119:169)

"My tongue shall speak thy word: for all thy commandments [Word] are righteousness." (Psalm 119:172)

"It is the spirit that quickeneth; the flesh profiteth nothing: the words that I speak unto you, they are spirit and they are life. But there are some of you who believe not." (John 6:63-64a KJV)

"It is the Spirit Who gives life [He is the Life-giver]; the flesh conveys no benefit whatever [there is no profit in it]. The words (truths) that I have been speaking to you are spirit and life. But [still] some of you fail to believe and trust and have faith." (John 6:63-64a AMP)

Brother, Sisters – be not among those who believe not.

CHAPTER 20

THE SECRET TO LIVING UNDER GRACE

Paul was a religious and literary genius. God used Paul's knowledge of the scriptures and gave Paul revelation so that he could deliver the mysteries of God to mankind. God turned a cold-blooded religious zealot and enemy of the Church into the revealer of the mysteries of God, *for the Church.*

Reading Paul's epistles carefully and intentionally, the finished work of Jesus is not just a mythological tale of old. The finished work of Jesus – His life, death, resurrection, and ascension to the right hand of the Throne of God; this becomes the full revelation of God's creation and salvation for mankind. Paul reveals the saga of mankind from the fall to victory; from separation from God, to holy reunion with the Father as Sons of God. All was made possible by the blood of the lamb – the Lamb of God, Jesus Christ.

This morning the Lord showed me the key words required for living under grace vs living under the law. In essence, these key words also brought a clearer understanding of faith. Hebrews 11:1 attempts to explain faith: **"Now faith is the substance of things hoped for, the evidence of things not seen."** To a new convert and to many multi-decade Christians, this explanation remains a mystery – beyond which their faith has not ventured. It sounds good in constant repetition, but the meaning has eluded millions for thousands of years.

What God showed me this morning is found in Romans 4:20-22:

"He [Abraham] staggered not at the promise of God through unbelief; but was strong in faith, giving glory to God;

And being fully persuaded that, what he has promised, he was able also to perform.

And therefore it was imputed [accounted] to him for righteousness."

The reader might say: "Sister Jannah, I've read this many times. I don't see the revelation in these words." Let me assist as the Holy Spirit assisted me.

Abraham, the Father of Faith, believed God despite all physical and natural signs pointing toward certain failure. Abraham did not stagger. To doubt God's promises is to stagger – often to stagger and fall. But Abraham staggered not. As old as he and Sarai were; as old as their bodies had become; as deteriorated as his and her physical organs had become – Abraham believed God. Abraham was **fully persuaded!**

Aha! There you have it! **Faith IS being fully persuaded** – despite how the circumstances look; despite what the scientists and doctors say; despite what the senses dictate. It's not easy! It goes against all we've learned in our many years of following the guidance of the senses – the fruit of the Tree of the Knowledge of Good and Evil. The serpent of logic still slithers alongside to whisper about the ridiculousness of faith, in the eyes of all these evidences to the contrary. God counted Abraham's full persuasion as righteousness. When we become fully persuaded that God's Word is true; when we become fully persuaded that every promise of God is true – despite how circumstances appear – God counts that as righteousness.

The secret to walking and living under grace is to be fully persuaded. You must be fully persuaded that Jesus paid the price for your redemption. You must be fully persuaded that all of your sins have been remitted [done away with as if they never existed]. You must be fully persuaded that you are the righteousness of God. You must be fully persuaded that you now have eternal life. You must be fully persuaded that God's nature of love now exists in you. You must be fully persuaded that you only now follow two commandments – commandments that embrace it all. You must be fully persuaded that you are sanctified. You must be fully persuaded that your carnal reasoning is of no avail here. You must be fully persuaded that hearing, reading, studying, meditating, and living the Word of God will renew your mind and thus your behavior. You must be fully persuaded that your ultimate goal is to live under the direction of the Holy Spirit.

And in case anyone thinks that this imputation of righteousness was for Abraham alone, let us read on in Romans 4:23-25:

"Now it was not written for his [Abraham's] sake alone, that it was imputed to him;

But for us also, to whom it shall be imputed, if we believe on him that raised up Jesus our Lord from the dead;

Who was delivered for our offences; and was raised again for our justification."

Romans 5:1-2 summarizes: "Therefore being justified by faith, we have peace with God through our Lord Jesus Christ.

By whom also we have access by faith into his grace wherein we stand, and rejoice in hope of the glory of God."

If we can become fully persuaded of our inheritance in Christ Jesus. If we can become fully persuaded that we no longer live under the Law of Sin and Death – but under the Law of the Spirit of Life in Christ Jesus. If we are fully persuaded that our slates are cleaned daily by repentance and God's forgiveness. If we are fully persuaded that we can approach the Throne of Grace in prayer without any guilt, shame, or condemnation. If we are fully persuaded that our duty is to become God's distributors of love on this earth. Then we live under grace. No more doubt. No more fear of hell fire.

A mundane example. Every year good working Christians and non-Christians work hard on their jobs. In the first quarter of the following year, they all file their income taxes – most hoping for a refund. It never really crosses the tax-filer's mind that Uncle Sam will not provide the refund computed. Each taxpayer is fully persuaded that the refund will come. Even though we have never really seen Uncle Sam in person; nor do we know his address – we are fully persuaded that the refund is due and will come.

How much more should we trust our unseen Father in heaven. He is not a man that He should lie.

Faith is being fully persuaded. Living under grace is being fully persuaded. Are you fully persuaded?

Read this book. Share it with Christian and non-Christian friends. Discuss grace. Pray to God to open your understanding to the freedom and liberty that Jesus Christ paid the price for. Ask God to reveal the fullness of the reality of redemption – the universe-level legal release of mankind from satan's oppression.

Pray this prayer:

Heavenly Father, I come to you in the name of Jesus Christ of Nazareth, thanking you for this book and its author – thanking you for Paul and the epistles that he wrote to unveil your mysteries to mankind. Father I ask that you open up these revelations in my mind, my heart, and my life.

Let me be the beacon of love, joy, and hope that you intended me to be in this world.

Father, let this message reach your remnant in today's Church so that the Body of Christ can be fully prepared for your return. Bless Your Church with unity and a full understanding of the power you have

placed within us individually and collectively. Let Your Church rise up into the manifestation of the Sons of God. Let every knee bow and every tongue confess that You are the one true God.

Thank you for replacing the dead spirit of old. Help me to always realize that I am saved by grace through faith. Father help me to maintain my spiritual position of being fully persuaded, no matter how the circumstances around me unfold. Let Your Holy Spirit keep me Father in thy place of grace, and love, and joy and peace.

Lord I am Your workmanship, created in Christ Jesus unto good works. Help me Father to always know and fulfill Your will.

In Jesus' Name. Amen.

REFERENCES AND RECOMMENDED READING

E.W. Kenyon, *New Creation Realities*, Kenyon's Gospel Publishing Society, Inc.: USA. (2011)

E.W. Kenyon, *The Blood Covenant*, Kenyon's Gospel Publishing Society, Inc.: USA. (1999)

Holy Bible KJV Reference Edition; Zondervan: Grand Rapids, MI, (1994)

Webster's Third New International Dictionary of the English Language Unabridged, Miriam-Webster Inc.: Springfield, MA. (1993)

Merriam-Webster's Collegiate Dictionary (11ᵗʰ Edition), Merriam-Webster, Inc.: Springfield, MA. (2006)

Prince, Derek, *By Grace Alone*, Chosen Books: Bloomington, MN, (2013)

cZondervan NIV Matthew Henry Commentary. Zondervan Publishing House: Grand Rapids, MI. (1992)

Strong, James, *The New Strong's Exhaustive Concordance of the Bible*. Comfort Print Edition. Thomas Nelson Publishers: Nashville, TN: (1995)

The Everyday Life Bible (Containing the Amplified Old Testament and the Amplified New Testament), Notes and commentary by Joyce Meyer. Faith Words: New York, NY. (1987)

Youngblood, Ronald F., General Editor, Nelson's New Illustrated Bible Dictionary. Nelson: Nashville, TN (1995)

Other Writings by Jannah A. Mitchell

Teaching Our Babies to Read (1993)

Like a Tree Planted (2006)

The Way from Darkness to Light (2015)

The Church 2016: State of the Union (2016)